Getting Real About
Having It All

Getting Real About Having It All

*Be your best,
love your career, and
bring back your sparkle*

Megan Dalla-Camina

Published and distributed in Australia by: Hay House Australia Pty. Ltd.: www.hayhouse.com.au
Published and distributed in the United States by: Hay House, Inc.: www.hayhouse.com
Published and distributed in the United Kingdom by: Hay House UK, Ltd.: www.hayhouse.co.uk
Published and distributed in South Africa by: Hay House SA (Pty), Ltd.: www.hayhouse.co.za
Distributed in Canada by: Raincoast: www.raincoast.com
Published in India by: Hay House Publishers India: www.hayhouse.co.in

Design by Rhett Nacson
Typeset by Simon Paterson
Edited by Margie Tubbs
Author photo by Jacqui Way Photograhy

ISBN: 978-1-4019-3849-9
Digital ISBN: 978-1-4019-3377-7

15 14 13 12   4 3 2 1
1st Australian edition, November 2012

Printed in Australia by McPherson's Printing Group

For women everywhere, who dream of a life overflowing with passion, career love, wellbeing and space to breathe. It's all waiting for you. May you find everything you are looking for.

AND

For Luca, my gorgeous boy. You are my greatest gift, and my greatest teacher. To the moon and back doesn't even begin to cover it.

Contents

Getting Real About Having It All

S o this is where we are. Really? Is this it? I know this is what many of us are thinking. After all the work, the effort, the sacrifices, and the lessons of those who have come before us, why haven't we figured it all out yet?

It's not as if it's that hard; working out how to have the career we want, while living the life we love, and being well in the process. Finding that miracle of work-life-balance. Discovering how to have the perfect relationship, while having the perfect hair, the power career, the angelic children, oh and of course, the line-free face and the killer figure. Haven't you sorted that out yet? Aren't we done already?

Sigh. Can't you just hear the collective sigh of a generation? Many generations. Amazing women, who have worked so hard, tried so hard, played by the rules (mostly) and achieved great success with more to come, but are still yet to arrive. And at what cost? What is the cost of all of this striving?

I look around at my contemporaries, women who are powerful in their own right; women who inspire and amaze me with all they do and all they have achieved; women who have started businesses while raising children and running charities and being good wives and sisters and daughters and employees. And while I marvel at their successes, for the most part I worry about the hidden, unspoken truth that lies just beneath. Because for many of us, it is the sheer exhaustion that comes with it all. Exhaustion from the striving, the struggling, the never-ending juggling. And the exhaustion that comes from the fear that maybe, just maybe, it will still never be enough.

And what does that mean? That even with all of the careful planning, the work and the sacrifices, it may still not be enough? Well, let's start with what is enough. For whom and by what measure? The measure that society places on success is so unachievable, so unattainable, that no amount of striving will ever get us there. We will always strive, never to arrive, and always to feel, if we are honest, just a little bit cheated.

So, have you had enough of this already? I know I have. It's time for a change. It's time to create positive change. And we are the only ones who can do it. We can no longer wait for the change to come. As Gandhi said, *we have to be the change.*

And so, if you are willing, it starts here with a new journey. This journey is one of empowerment. It is one of inspiration. It is a journey of understanding and releasing what may not have worked in the past, celebrating what is working in the present, and dreaming and planning what amazing things can be ahead in the future. As the poster on my wall says, *it's time to pull up your big girl panties and just get on with it!*

So what does 'just get on with it' look like, I hear you ask? It's time for us to create the lives we were born to live. Yes, I know that is all very Oprah of me, but she says it for a reason, right? We are the ones we have been waiting for. We are the ones who know ourselves, who can understand what we want; know what we are willing to give to get; know how we really want to balance work and play; know how we want to support our families and nurture our relationships. And we are the only ones who can really dream what our lives could look like, if only we are brave enough to hope for it.

I have written this book as a memo to generations of amazing, inspirational women who need a little support and nurturing, some encouragement to dare to dream, and to dare to plan that dream. Whether you are 25 or 45, single and starting out or married with four kids; working in a big corporation, a small government department, or running your own show; I hope this book can help you get from where you are today, to where you dream of being. I get asked all the time what 'having it all' looks like. I know what it looks like for me, but I can't define it for you. 'Having it all' is not a one stop shop. It is your choice. It is entirely up to you to decide what that looks like. You decide that part, and I'll happily and humbly be your guide and companion on the journey, and throw in the 'getting real' truth, to keep you on the path.

I'm not writing this book from a place of being an expert, or someone who is perfect and knows and does it all. I write it from a place of passion, of wanting to share my lessons, so that it may help and support you on your journey. We are not perfect. I most certainly am not. And we need not strive for perfection. Who needs that pressure, and it is not possible anyway! We just need to let ourselves be real, do the best we can or, as Wayne Dyer says, *just be*. Full stop. What else is there?

So, let's get busy and have some fun. This book is in three parts. Part One looks at bringing out your personal best so that you are coming from a place of personal knowing and strength. This is really the only place to build from, especially when building a strong career and a fulfilling personal life. Part Two looks at how to build and shape a career that you love, and it provides some of the tools and support you need to do that. And Part Three guides you in the right direction to create true wellbeing in your life. This is the part that most women I know struggle with. With so much else to do, the well woman in us all is often left wanting. Desperately. Actually, she is dying on the vine, let's be honest! Well, I say, enough already. It's time to nourish the Goddess, because if she isn't up to it, everyone else can just pack their bags right now and go on home!

I invite you to come on this wonderful journey with me. The best I am sure is yet to come, and you will create it. You just have to dare to dream, and then be prepared to do the work. Let's get started.

Megan xo

About me

I think it is a fair question to ask who I am, before going on this journey with me. I would, if I were you. You will read lots of juicy tales from my story throughout the book, but let me just give you a snapshot, so you know who I am and some of the experiences that have shaped me.

I have had all manner of jobs. Advertising agencies, a small music publishing business, insurance company, oh, and lots of fun time as a waitress in my younger years. But I have spent the majority of my career, the past 18 years or so, working in 'corporate America'. Big, successful companies like GE, PwC and IBM. I have travelled all over, and spent a lot of time working in the US, Asia, and my home base, Australia. It has been an amazing ride.

I dedicated a large part of my career to being the best marketer I could be, and that led me to run one of the biggest marketing organisations in the country, win a bunch of awards and be named one of Australia's most powerful marketers. Yep, that was pretty cool. I have also spent the best part of the last decade focused on strategies to empower and inspire women in business. More awards, shared the stage with the Prime Minister, got to speak at conferences all over, and met and worked with amazing feminist pioneers like Naomi Wolf. Not too shabby either.

I have worked for Senior Vice Presidents, managing people and projects in dozens of countries; provided counsel to CEOs in complex business environments; been part of senior leadership teams; and worked at the highest levels in business. Did I mention these were all in really-male dominated environments? Tick that box. Also tick the box for former workaholic, stress maddened, once chucked in the biggest job of my career due to illness, and complete burn out. Tick, tick, tick. Yep, lots of lessons there, my friends.

On the 'qualifications' front, I have a Masters degree in Business Management, as well as a Masters degree in Wellness, majoring in Positive Psychology. I am a yoga and meditation teacher, and have done a heap of work looking at what makes individuals thrive, and organisations successful. All relevant to our discussions. I can also sing you up a storm, perform Shakespeare, rock some ballet moves or produce you a music album if you like, being a qualified performer/dancer/dramarama/sound engineer and all – but maybe not so relevant to this book. Nope, don't think so – but some fun stories over a glass of wine for sure (not to mention the photos!).

On the life front (as if all of that isn't) I have seen all of this through many lenses – being single and fancy free; married with no kids; married with a kid; single working mother; living with partner working mother with teenage live-in stepkids; and back to single working mother again. So hopefully, I can kind of relate to many of the situations you may find yourself in. Been there, done that, got the T-shirt.

And maybe the most important part of shaping who I am today, and my perspectives on the world, is that I have been on a journey from illness, chaos and despair, to health, wellbeing, happiness and, dare I say it, balance. So I can share some of those learnings with you too.

I think the most important thing you can know up front, is that I have lived every single word in this book. I have experienced it all and have come out the other side. And it is my greatest passion in life to share what I have learnt, so that others may have a smoother path. I hope that is the case for you, and I hope you enjoy the journey.

How to use this book

My intention for this book is for it to be a guiding light for you. You can turn it on when you need it, and when you don't, you are safe in the knowledge that you always know where the switch is. I would love it to be like your really smart best friend – the one who is always there, always has really good answers, and points you in the right direction. She also knows how to give you just the right kind of hug, and yes, she will kick you up the ass when you need it too (gently and with love, of course).

You may choose to dive straight in and read this book from cover to cover. If you feel so inclined, hey go for it. Or you may choose to dip in and out as the mood takes you, choosing to read a chapter here and there, as issues surface or your curiosity is aroused about a particular topic. You might like to write down your thoughts in a journal, make notes in the page margin, or doodle to your heart's content. That is all just fine too.

This book is not meant to be hard work. It is intended to be a journey of self-discovery into the essence of who you are, and how you can best show up in the world. Lean into it. Feel your way. Go where you are moved to go. One day that might be on a meditation adventure, and the next might be on setting those boundaries or creating your life vision. There are no rules. There is only my heartfelt wish that my words might shine a light on your path, and that they may in some small way, illuminate your journey.

Bringing Out Your Personal Best

Don't compromise yourself. You are all you've got.

– Janis Joplin

Here we go. Part One. This part of the book is all about you. How often do you hear that? Rarely, I would guess. We are going to look at how to bring out your best, the best of who you are. Who you *already* are. It's not about changing you, or becoming something you're not, or living up to someone else's expectation of you or what your life should look like. It's about you. The real you. I hope it will give you a place and some space to breathe, and to journey back and reconnect with some of the fundamentally wonderful things about who you really are.

We will ask some pretty powerful questions, and seek out the answers together. Questions like *what are you passionate about?* Hmmm, I wonder when was the last time someone asked you that. *What do you want for your life?* We will look at your values and discover your strengths. You will learn how to be here now, and how to focus your attention. We will talk about crazy things like setting boundaries and figuring out what your non-negotiables are (say *what?*). Yes, we will. And we will look at the power of creating positive change and, wait for it, getting happy.

Oh my, we are going to be busy. We will do all of this and more, and we will do it with grace and ease. We will hold it lightly and have a laugh. And we will go on a journey of discovery and contemplation into how you really want to show up in the world. And then you will go create it.

How wonderful. Are you up for it? I know you are. Let's begin.

CHAPTER 1

Follow your passion

*Follow what you are genuinely passionate about
and let that guide you to your destination.*

– Diane Sawyer

Wow, first topic off the bat and we are going to talk about just a small thing. Passion. Couldn't I have picked a slightly smaller thing to get into first? You know, warm us both up a little? Well no, actually. I put this chapter first because I think it is so important, and so completely foundational to thriving. So it comes before all the others for a reason.

Our passions define us, they tell the world who we are, and what we care about, and they can make the difference between a life just lived, or a life fulfilled. Our passions ignite us, they get the fire burning somewhere deep down in our souls, and they make us want to leap out of bed in the morning and stay up all night. They make us come alive.

We all know what it feels like when we are engaged in something that we are passionate about. We feel alive, energised, filled with excitement and we never want it to end. You know the feeling – you get those butterflies in your stomach and you can't sit still – like when you first met that hot guy, who would later become your husband. Like how you feel when you kick off that amazing project you have been dreaming about, and that you just can't stop thinking about.

It's about how you feel when you start to write that book, paint that picture, compose that song or teach that child to read. That's passion. We also know what it's like when we're lacking passion. Your energy is low, you're unproductive, and you just want to lie down and take a big ol' nap. No-one wants to live like that, at least no-one who is awake, sane and has a choice.

I am assuming that you are awake, sane and have a choice, or you probably wouldn't have picked up my book. So what does following your passion mean? Well, let's first look at what it doesn't look like. It doesn't look like being stuck and consumed totally in the monotonous, everyday jobs and must-do lists, that we all have to deal with. Of course they exist, but they don't have to rule our universe, unless we choose to let them.

Our lives become what we think about most. When we are standing in our power, inspired and living with passion, we are functioning on a different energetic level. We are alive. Thriving. We have our glow on. And not only do we feel it, but everyone around us feels it too. You know when you come into contact with those people in your day, the ones whose energy is just contagious. They're infectious and you just want to spin in their orbit. Well, I would bet that they are living their passion, and it is radiating out to the world. It's a beautiful thing to witness, and we should want that for ourselves. Why not? Why shouldn't we live our lives like that?

Now, before you go all 'but I have a job, a boyfriend, and a mother to take care of, bills and a mortgage and college fees to repay, and don't even talk to me about the kids ...' Stop. I get it. We all live in the real world. I get that. I am here with you in what can sometimes feel like a never-ending barrage of reality. And sometimes it sucks and it can be all-consuming.

But that is not our entire existence. The more we can live from a place of passion, the more we can rise up above the everyday muck, and live inspired lives. If I can do it (at least some of the time), I know you can too.

I can relate to the nay-sayers among you, as I have lived a life where there was no room for passion, or at least I didn't think there was. You will hear stories from my journey throughout the book. And you will come to learn that there was a time in my life when I was so consumed with my job, and meeting everyone's expectations except my own, that I thought there was no space, time or energy for my passions. And in fact, I was right, because I hadn't stopped (or even paused) long enough to consider what my passions were, or if indeed I was living them. I thought I was. I was doing my dream job, or what I thought was my dream job. And I was working myself into the ground, proving to everyone that I could do it.

But when I look back, it was not passion that was driving me. It was actually fear. Fear of failure. Fear of not being enough. Not smart enough, not capable enough, just not good enough. And you cannot live in a place of passion if you are consumed by fear. It just can't happen. It took me a long time to work out what my passion was at that point in my life. It took going down a few different paths to get on the right one. And that's okay. The important thing is being on the path, even if it's just the path of discovery to find the right one.

So what can we do, to actually get on the path? Well, I'm glad you asked. Here are three key ways you can live with more passion in your life, starting right now.

···· What do you absolutely love to do?

What moves you most? What do you love? What lights your fire? Sounds like an easy question, but sometimes it's not so simple to answer. And it changes too. What you were totally passionate about a year ago may not be what floats your boat today.

It's important to spend some time really sitting with this question. We're not looking for a superficial answer; we're looking for the true, deep and inspiring passion, that drives, motivates and consumes you. And you may have to get really still and quiet and think for a while, to tap into that. That's okay; we have all the time in the world.

For me, passion is about creating positive change in the world. It's about speaking, coaching and writing books that inspire and empower people to live amazing lives. It's about inspiring organisations to do great things and be a place of empowerment and engagement. It's about amazing, positive leadership. A decade ago, it was running marketing for major multinational companies. A decade before that, it was acting and performing on the stage. It changes. And that's fine. The important thing is that you move with the change, that you are aware of it, and that you don't get stuck living a life and following a passion that you have long outgrown, and that just doesn't fit you anymore.

···• It's not all about work

Who said that all of our passions need to be fulfilled through our paid work? Let's be clear – following your bliss doesn't mean you have to send your whole life into complete upheaval. Sure, in an ideal world your day job would be the thing that totally rocks your world. Some wise person once said that *if you do what you love and get paid for it, you would never work a day in your life.* I am sure that is true. But it is not possible for everyone who has to earn a living, certainly not all of the time.

But that doesn't mean that you can't have passion in your life, and that you can't live a fulfilled life. Passion can be found in all sorts of places, and it is unique to everyone. Your passion might be public speaking, negotiating deals or making a sale. Or it could be playing the guitar, singing in a band, collecting china dolls, or writing poetry. It could come out in your day job, or it could be something that you ignite on the evenings or weekends. It doesn't matter. It only matters that you tap into it as often as you can. And if your paid work is not the source of your passion, try and find ways to incorporate small parts (or big parts) into your job, to light that fire more often.

···• Make time to make it work

This is key. Time. Making time to make it work. It is great to identify your passion, and work out how you can incorporate your passion into your life. But if you don't make time for it, it is all just an academic exercise. And that doesn't get you far. You have to work out when, where and how it will happen. We will be talking about strengths, goals as well as time and energy management in the following chapters, which will all help you to follow through on making it work. We will also cover creating space, which for many of us is a critical step, so we actually have some breathing space to focus on what matters.

Having what we want in our lives starts with getting real about who we are and what we are passionate about. It starts here. So, if you feel like it, spend some time on this before you move on. Then you will have a strong foundation and perspective on what really matters most: where you come alive, and what you need, to truly live a passionate life.

Getting real – *try this*

···• Take some time to discover what your passion is now, not what it may have been yesterday, last week, or last year. Think about these questions: If you were stuck in a book shop overnight, which section would you sleep in? When you think of doing something, what do you get really excited about? If you had a week off work, and you could spend the time doing something you absolutely loved, what would it be? If you were at a fabulous dinner party, who would you want to sit next to and what would you talk about? Think about these questions – they may help you find the spark.

···• Determine how you can incorporate more of what you are passionate about into your day. Look at your friends, colleagues or role models who have done this effectively. See what has worked for them, and try it too.

···• Make time. Have the intention to live your most passionate life, and put things in place to make it happen. Then watch your world change.

CHAPTER 2

Create a life vision

Open your eyes, look within.
Are you satisfied with the life you're living?

– Bob Marley

D o you have a vision for your life? A vision for how you want your life to look like a month, year or decade from now? Huh? What's that I hear you ask? Well, that just about sums it up for so many women (and men, I might add) that I speak to.

Some people have a career plan, and we will talk about that in Part Two of this book. And when you go to see a coach or have a meeting with a prospective employer, many times the career plan gets a look-in. You know the questions. Where will you be in a few years? In ten years? What is your career aspiration? Where does this role fit in your overall plan? And so on. But they are asking about your job. Not your life. And how could you possibly know what your career should look like, if you don't have a clear vision of what you want your life to look like?

Well, I don't think that you can.

When I talk about a life vision, I'm talking about having a clear view of how everything in your life fits together in your ideal picture. It's about what your dream existence looks like. It's about your aspirational picture. And it includes everything, things like:

···• career
···• relationships
···• passions
···• friends
···• hobbies
···• travel
···• study
···• charitable pursuits
···• home environment
···• community involvement
···• what your lifestyle looks like
···• where you want to live
···• type of person you want to be
···• spiritual life
···• having kids/not having kids
···• family life
···• health and wellbeing
···• your bucket list

I know it's a long list! But so many people get to middle age – you know, over 40 (middle age – really?), and then sit back, take a long and sometimes hard look, and wonder what on earth happened (actually, the language is usually a little more colourful!). Maybe you have been there, are worried you could be there one day, or know someone who has been. Well, I say 'no thanks' to feeling like you hadn't lived the way you wanted to, when it was in your power the whole time to do just that. Hands down for that! So let's look at what we can do, and let me share a little of my colourful story to help smooth the process.

···• **Creating the vision**

For the first half of my life, my vision was to be an actress – actually, scratch that – my vision was to be a *movie star*. I wanted the big kahuna. I didn't really think too much about what my whole life looked like; I just saw the big prize. Now for many reasons the big prize never eventuated, and I will go into that later in the book. And you will hear lots of my big, juicy, messy, crazy story (oh dear!). After that vision fizzled into a big dried-up old prune, I spent many years, about a decade in fact, not having much of a life vision, other than working like a mad woman, and running myself into the ground in the process. I thought I was happy in this vision, but I was really just on that treadmill, running fast for fear of falling off.

And then, thankfully, one day I did fall off. And then I woke up. But this was no *Sleeping Beauty* story. I woke up sick, tired, overworked, overwhelmed, and with very little life to speak of. As my mother said to me on a pivotal day in my life, when I chucked in the biggest and most important job I had ever had (yep, more on that later too), 'Megan, you have no life – you just have a job'. Bam! In a nutshell – don't you just love how mothers do that?

So what changed for me on that day, and in the days and months to follow? Well, pretty simply put, I worked out what I wanted my life to look like. Sounds simple, but it's a little more involved than just snapping your fingers and saying *twinkle, twinkle fix my life*. But after sitting myself down and getting serious (lovely conversation), I realised that I wanted my life to look something like this:

1. Actually have a life – crazy concept, I know.

2. Be healthy and well, not just dragging my tired, old (but fabulous) ass from day to day, just trying to get through it.

3. Have real time to spend with Luca, my son, who was five at the time (which, just so you know, involved things like being home two to three days a week when he came home from school, to hang out, do homework, bake cookies – you know, that cool Mum

stuff. Actually, the cookies thing still hasn't happened, but he lives in hope).

4. Do meaningful work that is purposeful and fulfilling. Balance the amount of time and energy I invest in my work pursuits, with the time and energy I give to Luca and everything else on my list.

5. Have real time for my family and friends, not just include them as a squeezed in, stressed out afterthought.

6. Enjoy my hobbies, like reading and writing.

7. Pursue my passions – actually, I had to rediscover what they were, as we went through in Chapter 1. I did, and here we are (writing, this book and more to follow, wellness, study, meditation, yoga ... the list goes on).

8. Have a calm, peaceful home life; not a rushed, crazy, stress-filled madhouse.

9. Travel and spend real time in my favourite places – like New York and Byron Bay.

10. Be happy and enjoy living my life.

There you have it. I can happily, honestly say that today, I am pretty much living my vision. Of course I have days, or even weeks and months sometimes, when the ship gets skewed off course (and yes, I have been shipwrecked once or twice since I started). But generally speaking, I am living the life I envisioned when it all went to hell in a handbasket. I created it. And you can too. If I can get to where I am, from where I was, which felt like a really dark place, I truly believe anyone can. You just have to spend the time to create your vision, and then you have to want it enough to work for it.

···• Chart your course

This section of the book is all about you. Well, the whole book is all about you (don't you just love that). But this section is about bringing out the best in you, so you can thrive in your career, and in your whole life. We are going to talk about many of the things that will help you chart your course to the life you want to live and, importantly, how you want to live it.

The *how* is so incredibly important. There is so much information out there about *what* to do. But there is very little real, helpful, inspire-you-to-action information about how to actually do it. Hopefully this is where my book can help.

We will talk about values, strengths, being mindful, setting boundaries and knowing what your non-negotiables are, so you can live your vision, not just dream about it. And we will talk about how to actually create the change you are longing for, not just think about it.

So, before we get in to all of that (you might want to grab a cup of tea), I would love it if you had some quiet time, to sit with a pen and paper and dream about what your life vision looks like. I must confess right now, that I hate the part in so many books, when they tell you it's time to get your journal out, or they have those little lines where you can write down all of your innermost thoughts on five teeny tiny lines. I know it all sounds a little hokey, but it doesn't have to be. Think about it. This is your life. Your one and only life. Don't you think you deserve the chance to make it exactly what you want it to be, even if it makes you a little uncomfortable going through the process?

I think you deserve it, and you are worth it. Of course you are. So, before moving on to the next chapter, have a think about what your list looks like. Mine at the time seemed completely unattainable. I might as well have been saying to myself 'wake up tomorrow, looking like Cindy Crawford'. But my list and image for my life evolved over time, and gradually it became my reality. It is not a grandiose list. It is pretty simple. Yours might be revolutionary. It doesn't matter. It's your vision, it's your life, and you create it. And we start from where we are. So start here.

Getting real – *remember*

···• This is a vision for your life, not your career. So please don't fill it up with all your work stuff. We will get to that. Take this time to really think about your whole life, and your dream vision. We will get into the reality stuff soon enough, so enjoy staying here for a brief moment in time.

···• Don't panic. It's actually kind of fun to take time out and fuel those creative juices. Build a vision board if you are a 'pictures' person – I actually have a vision wall in my home study that inspires me about the life I want to live, every time I sit down to work. Go and use a cool online tool, like Pinterest, to build vision boards in different areas of your life – you can check mine out while you are there (warning, it's completely addictive). Write down words in crayon, if you are a 'words' person. Or just write a list. It doesn't matter how you do it, just find the method that works for you.

···• Breathe and enjoy the process. And remember, it's your life. If you don't create your vision for yourself, trust me, someone else will. So it might as well be you. What are you waiting for?

CHAPTER 3

Know your values

It's not hard to make decisions
when you know what your values are.

– Roy Disney

Our values are our enduring beliefs, attitudes and behaviours, that are the core of our being and represent who we are. Wow, that sounds really serious doesn't it? It's not so scary really – just think of your values as your internal guidance system: your personal GPS, that provides direction and keeps you on track. Hopefully, they don't steer you in the wrong direction, as my car GPS does so often – no dead-ends on this journey I promise you!

Values tell the world who we are and what is important to us. Often when we are happiest and most fulfilled in our life, we are living in a way that is aligned with our values. We don't always set goals and demonstrate behaviours that are congruent with them, but when we do, we live a life filled with satisfaction, meaning and optimally, pleasure. These are all keys to a happy life, keys to the good life. Most importantly though, is that when we are following a path that is in keeping with our values, we don't do silly stuff that doesn't satisfy us, because we know that it doesn't fit with what really matters. And that can save us from a world of pain, and lead us into a world of joy – and we all want that.

For us to live purposeful lives, it is key that we understand and can clearly articulate the things that are most important to us. Do you know what your values are? Could you list them down on paper if I asked you to? (Get ready, your time is coming.) We are directed by our values with the choices we make every day. Personally, my values direct the bulk of my decisions, both big and small, conscious and unconscious: which people and groups will I associate with, which food will I eat, where will I live, who will I date, what clothes will I buy, where will I send my son to school, and which organisation will I work for? Take my work for example – I make a value choice everyday I show up for work in my organisation, as my values are very clearly aligned to the values of the company. I couldn't work there otherwise. But not everyone can say that, mostly because not everyone knows what their values are.

Taking the time and thought to articulate your values can be an empowering exercise, that can direct the way you live your life. An inspiring mentee of mine, Holly Ransom, turned up to one of our sessions with some documents to discuss. One of them was a list of goals (about 80 of them I might add; I nearly died, but more on that in a later chapter), and the other contained her stated values. I have to tell you I was blown away. I had never seen anyone have such a clear and crisply articulated sense of who they were. Holly's values provided such clarity on how they were directing her life's purpose. Oh, did I add that Holly was 21 at the time? It was astounding to me. When I was 21, I was so busy running around working and playing hard, that I didn't have a clue what my values were or where they could have been directing me. As it turned out, I was directed straight to bed with chronic fatigue syndrome for six months, which might have been a hint that I wasn't living an aligned life. You think?

I was so impressed with Holly's values, I asked for her permission to share them with you. What struck me most was that it is not just a list of nouns: you know, leadership, gratitude, kindness etc. The depth of her articulation on what each value means to her, and how it plays out in her life, is what is really special here.

···· Holly Ransom's values

1. **Integrity** – I live life according to the fundamental components of my being: my core values and principles. There can be no happiness and no true success achieved in a life lived to any other standard. I always say what I mean and I always do what I say.

2. **Loyalty** – Life, put simply, is a multitude of relationships. The foundation of strong relationships and the highest form of human motivation is trust. Loyalty is fundamental to developing and sustaining the relationships that will enrich my life.

3. **Hard work** – The only place where success comes before work is in the dictionary. There is no substitute for hard work ... if it was easy, it would have been done already. I get out of life what I am prepared to put in, so I always put it all in.

4. **Empathy** – I seek first to understand, then to be understood. I walk a mile in the shoes of others, before I offer opinion or advice. I choose to let my empathy be demonstrated not by thought, but by action.

5. **Extra mile leadership** – No-one has ever attained eminent success by simply doing what is required of them. I always go the extra mile, because the little things in life mean everything. And that little bit 'extra' is the difference between ordinary and extraordinary.

6. **Unselfishness** – I willingly sacrifice my personal interests or glory for the welfare of others. Each and every day, I strive to do something to help someone who'll never be able to repay me.

7. **Respect** – Everyone matters: nobody deserves anything less than my utmost respect for their beliefs, traditions, culture, feelings and opinions. Self-respect guides my morals; respect for others guides my manners. I cannot truly respect others, unless I respect myself.

8. **Gratefulness** – I never take anything or anyone in life for granted. I will continually express and demonstrate my gratitude to those who have enriched my life, for I can only be said to be alive in those moments, when my heart is truly conscious of its treasures.

9. **Positive attitude** – nothing great was ever accomplished without enthusiasm. I have the choice to make my day a 1/10 or a 10/10 day, and I choose 10/10 every day. What I believe, I will become; what I visualise, I will create; and what I focus on expands. So I think positive and dream big.

10. **Courage** – It takes courage to believe that anything is possible, and even more courage to devote my life to making those possibilities happen, and to acting despite the negativity and doubt springing from those who still have 'impossible' in their vocabulary. I have the courage to jump and the faith to know that the net will catch me.

How inspiring is that? I hope you can see why I was totally blown away. I share these in full, hoping that they may inspire you to create your own, or think more deeply about them if you feel you need to. Now, creating values looks different for everyone. You might have ten like Holly, or you might have three core values that you live your life by. The number of them doesn't matter; the intent behind them, and how you live by them, is what counts.

While our behaviours may not always be completely in line with our values – I value wellness, but will still sometimes eat a cupcake or three – the fact that we have them, are aware of them, and can use them to direct us towards our best life, is what is most meaningful. And the more we can live our lives in line with the things that we value the most, the happier and more fulfilled we will be.

Getting real – *try this*

···• List the things you value most in your life. If this is difficult for you, think about how you would like others to view you, or how you want to be remembered. You can also think about people you admire and why. This may give you some clues as to what is really important for you.

···• How closely is your life currently aligned to your values? Do a stocktake of where you are, and are not, aligned. Think about the obstacles to living your values, any resistance you may face, and how to counter it.

···• Take action – identify what actions you can take to make your life more aligned, starting with small actions and also thinking about bigger actions you can take, if you feel this is necessary.

CHAPTER 4

Use your strengths

*We are each gifted in a unique and important way. It is our
privilege and our adventure to discover our own special light.*

– Mary Dunbar

So many women spend a massive amount of time and energy worrying about what is wrong with them – their problems, stressors and all of the struggles. Not to mention the fretting we do over what we think are our personal flaws, from the physical to the psychological and everything in between. No wonder we get headaches! But there is more to life than thinking and focusing on our perceived problems. Science is showing us that, by focusing on our strengths instead of our weaknesses, we can go from a life filled with what's wrong, to a life that is strong. And who wouldn't want a piece of that?

We all have character strengths: thoughts, feelings and behaviours that feel authentic to us and come naturally. Your strengths are unique to you, and you feel energised and alive when you use them. They are also things that, when utilised, take us into flow. You know what flow is, right? It's that brilliant experience, when we get the right mix between using our strengths and the challenge of the task, and using our strengths gets us there. They get us into the sweet spot, that place when we feel we are at our best, getting the most enjoyment out of what we do, where things feel juicy. It is also where we have the greatest opportunity to grow, and where we feel intrinsically (internally) rewarded for what we do. Pretty cool, huh!

But here's the downside: research shows us that very few of us actually get to do what we do best every day. How sad is that? We also know from the research that when we don't get to use our strengths, we are less likely to be engaged at work, less likely to be happy in our personal lives, and generally will have a lower life satisfaction. So stop the bus, it's time to sort this out right now.

So how do we get to use our strengths? Well first, we need to know what they are (duh). One of the greatest challenges, when actually using your strengths, is identifying them. Many women are so used to underplaying what is good about them that thinking about their strengths can seem like a huge mountain to climb.

···· Identifying our strengths

So where to start? You can work at identifying your strengths yourself, by spending some time thinking about the areas in your life where you get most enjoyment. Think about the things that really bring you alive, that drive your zest for life. They could be things like learning, showing gratitude to others, being curious, being kind, being a leader or showing love. Spend some time exploring what these could look like for you, and where in your day they have the chance to shine.

If you are still struggling, then enlist a friend who knows you really well to help you. Ask your friend to name three or more of your strengths, and see what comes up. You might be surprised. You could even speak to a range of people – friends, family, colleagues – to gain different opinions, and then see what resonates the most. Be careful not to just throw things out instantly, without considering them properly. What may at first seem ridiculous, on closer consideration might uncover something deeper about yourself, or something that you had long since buried.

There are also some great tools around that you can have a play with, that will identify your strengths for you. The one I like and use the most in my work is the *Values In Action* survey. At the website www.viame.org, you can find a range of tools to help you identify your strengths. You can complete a survey called the *VIA Inventory of Strengths* survey. This is a 240-item assessment tool, which has been developed scientifically to measure a person's character strengths. It has been used more than 1.3 million times worldwide, and is available in 17 languages, so you know it is robust. And there are adult and youth versions of the survey, so you can play with this with the whole family – it's a fascinating discussion to have with your kids, or nieces, nephews and friends.

According to the *VIA Institute*, a strengths-based approach to life:

···• **Is honest** – acknowledges problems, but doesn't get lost in them

···• **Is positive** – focuses on what is best and good

···• **Is empowering** – encourages and advances the individual

···• **Is energising** – uplifts and fuels the person

···• **Is connecting** – brings the person closer to others, aiding in mutual connection

Knowing your personal character strengths – what's best about you as a human being – is powerful knowledge, that can be used to reach your full potential with your work, your family and your relationships.

···• How do we use our strengths?

Once we have identified our strengths, we need to work out how to get more of that juice in our days and weeks, because we know we will thrive when we do. So think about new and interesting ways you can use your strengths every day.

You might like to choose your top three *VIA* signature strengths, and then for a month at a time, focus on just one. Think of a project you have going on at work, and use your top strength to tackle it differently. Or think of a situation with a family or friend that may be causing you a challenge, and employ your strength in a new way to work through that. If one of your strengths is love of learning, then pick up a new book on a topic you are interested in or research it on the Internet. If one of your top strengths is love, then think about how you express love for your family and friends and think of a new way to do that – it could be cooking a special meal, or just spending extra time together. Make sure, at the end of your experiment, you take time to think and write down how you felt about it – did you experience flow while performing a task in this way using your strength? We know from research that writing it down ensures the experience is more enjoyable, so take time to follow through with this.

A final word on strengths is around growth. We get the most growth when we are strongest. And as most of us want growth, I leave you with a quote from Marcus Buckingham in his book *Now, Discover Your Strengths*. Marcus is an absolute superstar of the strengths movement, and he has done decades of research on the subject. Here is what he says about strengths and growth: *You grow most in your areas of greatest strength. You will improve the most, be the most creative, be the most inquisitive, and bounce back the fastest in those areas where you have already shown some natural advantage over everyone else – your strengths. This doesn't mean you should ignore your weaknesses. It just means you'll grow most where you're already strong.*

Love it. You will be amazed, once you bring awareness to your strengths, how you can use them in your everyday life, and what a difference it will make to you when you do.

Getting real – *remember*

···• Write a list of your personal strengths as you see them, or ask a friend or family member what they think your strengths are.

···• Take a strengths questionnaire to get a scientific look at your strengths. My favourite is the *VIA Signature Strengths* tool, which you can find online at www.viame.org (and it's completely free).

···• Look at different ways you can use your strengths over the next three months. Pick your top three strengths, and use them in new and interesting ways, one each month, to see what difference it makes to your satisfaction and happiness levels. Try it – it works.

CHAPTER 5

Learn to be here now

Breathe. Let go. And remind yourself that this very
moment is the only one you know you have for sure.

– Oprah Winfrey

While writing this chapter, I am on vacation with my family in Banff, Canada. Yesterday afternoon, I had the chance to spend a few hours alone at the spa and go to the mineral pool, have a steam and a relaxing massage. This is my idea of complete and utter heaven. While I was lying on the massage table having an incredible therapist work on my very tight and tired shoulders, made more so by the 25 hours I had travelled to get here (yep, shocker), I was thinking about this chapter in the book, and all the wonderful things I could share that would help you to be present and live mindfully. And of course, I completely missed the point of all my wisdom, because while I was lying there being massaged, I wasn't really there at all – I was here with you, thinking about writing about being present. The irony did not escape me.

We spend so much of our lives being anywhere but here. Or thinking about anything but what we are currently doing. We are vacant in our own lives, ghosts living in the machine of our bodies, and we are missing it all. We could, in fact, be having the time of our lives, yet we wouldn't know it, as we simply aren't present. Does this sound like an exaggeration? It may, but if you did a little exercise tomorrow, and at the end of the day looked back and thought about how many moments you were truly present, conscious, actively engaged in what was happening moment by moment, you might just be surprised by how little you actually experienced.

In this book, we are talking about many things. But at the core of it, we are talking about creating our best lives. Lives we want to live. And to do that, we need to learn to be present.

Learning to be here now is all about learning to be mindful. Mindfulness brings our awareness to the present moment, to what we are doing and feeling right now. The greatest benefits are found when we practise this moment by moment, not just in a meditation practice. Cultivating our inherent, natural mindfulness has proven benefits for our health, happiness and relationships; and it allows us to bring more of our skills, strengths and authenticity into everything that we do.

In his beautiful book, *The Miracle of Mindfulness*, Thich Nhat Hanh writes about cultivating mindfulness through being present in everyday, sometimes mundane activities, like washing the dishes. Now I have never been a domestic goddess (just ask my ex-husband). But I can now appreciate and even enjoy the simple process of filling the sink with warm sudsy water, cleaning the dishes slowly while feeling the suds on my skin, rinsing the dishes and placing them on the rack to dry. In fact, it can even be a nice little respite from the busy-ness of the household, like a mini meditation in action.

Learning to be here now applies to all aspects of your life, and all moments. It applies to the current job role you are in. We will talk about creating your career in the next section. But as we think about mindfulness, think about how often you are fully present in your day-to-day work life. Are you actively engaged in the work you are doing, the people you are working with, and the projects you need to deliver? Or are you thinking about the next job you are going to get, the next pay rise, the next special project, and your career plan five years from now?

Anytime you are trying to get somewhere, other than where you are, you are not fully here. And when you are not here, you miss so much. Too much. It's really hard to build the career you want, to really excel at your work, if you are not fully present. We will explore this more later, but I plant the seed here because it is so relevant to this discussion, and bears thinking about.

It also applies to your relationships, whether that is with your immediate family, your kids, your boss, romantic partner or friends. When you come home from a day at work, where are you? Are you at home getting dinner ready, talking about your day, finding out about your kid's or partner's day, enjoying this time together? Or are you still at the office, buried in the issues of the week, worrying about that meeting tomorrow, and all the work you have to do later tonight to prepare for it? Yep, I know where you are. And you may as well still be at the office.

So how can we craft the skill of mindfulness, build the muscle so to speak? We practise mindfulness meditation. Chapter 25 covers meditation in detail: the why, when and how of building a meditation practice. Mindfulness meditation is in a different form. Instead of carving out specific time to sit on our meditation cushion with our eyes closed, when practising mindfulness all we need to do is just start being present and aware of what we are experiencing with what is going on around us. We can do this as we sit at our desk at work, as we walk down the street noticing the trees and birds, walking past the bakery that has the amazing fresh bread baking and enjoying the smell, or driving in our car to the office. It doesn't matter where you are or what you are doing – practising mindfulness throughout your day is about being in the moment, fully aware of what is happening, and experiencing all of it.

To explore more on how to build mindfulness, get a copy of *The Miracle of Mindfulness* by Thich Nhat Hanh. I would also recommend you read some books or watch some videos of Jon Kabat-Zinn, PhD, who is considered to be the father of mindfulness. His audiobook,

Mindfulness for Beginners, is a great starting place, and he has many more books and videos available for you to enjoy. Check out my website for all the details.

Getting real – *try this*

···• Today before you go to bed, think back at how many mindful moments you had during the day. Were there many? Did you go through the day on autopilot? Be honest with yourself, and perhaps write down your observations.

···• This week, choose three things that you do everyday, and do them mindfully. This could be brushing your teeth, doing the dishes, or making a cup of tea. Be fully present in the process, noticing every sensation, sound, smell, taste and touch.

···• Practise mindfulness meditation to enhance your skill at being in the present moment. Through practising meditation you will bring these skills into your everyday life.

CHAPTER 6

Focus your attention

Be a master of mind, rather than mastered by mind.

– Zen proverb

This could be one of the hardest chapters in this entire book for me to write. Not because I don't know anything about the science of attention, but because I am not an expert (by any stretch) at the art of applying it. Let me explain. I can be the mistress of procrastination and distraction. In fact, I am the queen of both. Now this is something I have down to a fine art. Take this book for example. Writing a book, as anyone who has done will attest, is no small thing. You have to be super focused, disciplined and dedicated to sitting alone at your computer (or note-book) day after day, night after night, to write your brilliant, poetic, insightful words on to the page (well, here's hoping they are). Now, that would be fine, if it weren't for one small thing – complete inability to focus. To give you some insight, this is what my writing process looks like, when I am at my most distracted:

> Sit down to write. Write one paragraph. Check *Twitter*. Tweet a few lines, retweet, and respond to comments. Make myself refocus. Write half a page. Look at *Facebook*, post a comment, scroll through posts. Back to the book, write another page or

two (if I am lucky), then flick over to play with my website for a few minutes. Check my *Blackberry*. Get up to go to the bathroom. Get a cup of tea. Unload the dishwasher. Flick through a magazine. Pull. My. Hair. Out.

Oh yes, this is what it can be like. Now, some of this *is* the writing process. Many writers will tell you that they will do anything they can, to stop having to actually sit down and commit words to paper. But most of it is just down to flat out distraction, and the pure inability to focus attention for any period of time. Frustrating? You bet. Common? Absolutely. Curable? Just maybe. Let's investigate.

We might think that we should be able to hold our attention and focus; we're not children after all. But *should* is a big word, especially when we don't really know what we are talking about. If you want to speak to someone who actually knows something about the art of focus, then you would speak to a neuroscientist (that's not me, just so you know). If you speak to a neuroscientist about the art of attention, they will likely speak to you about attention as an organ system. Like our circulatory system or our digestion, it is not a single function. Here is where the complication starts. The attention system, with its own anatomy, physiology and chemistry, actually has three types of attention within it: awareness or sensitivity to our surroundings; focus, or the spotlight of the mind; and executive judgement, skills relating to planning and judgement. See, not so simple after all – no wonder we find it so challenging to control.

But no matter how challenging, mastering our attention span is critical to our success, whether it be at home or at work, because it is our ticket to being able to focus on our goals, without being driven crazy by distraction. Our attention fuels our self-discipline, and it enables us to, you know, *think*. Kind of important wouldn't you say?

But still, so many of us, so much of the time, just cannot master it. So let's look at some of the reasons, and what you can do to kick your brain into one gear, instead of 5,000.

···· The myth and the reality of multi-tasking

Okay, so many of us think that we are just great at multi-tasking. We lord it over our male counterparts that we, almighty woman, the greater sex, can do more than one thing at a time, and they just simply cannot. How great are we! Well, we are great, of course. But not because of this. I hate to be the one to break it to you, but this myth that we can multi-task, and be effective at the same time, is kind of not true. Actually, it's a flat out lie. Let me explain.

Our brains like to focus. Think about it. You may think you are being effective when you are responding to an email, while being on a conference call, sending a tweet, watching your kids do their homework, cooking dinner on the stove while having a face mask on and drying your nail polish (oh, yes I have). But your brain is freaking out, and you are actually taking so much more time to get things done than if you did them sequentially, instead of all (unsuccessfully) at the same time. You are in fact not multi-tasking; you are doing what I call micro switching – switching from one thing to another, at tiny intervals, constantly. And unless you are in the rare minority who can do this effectively, you are simply, well, not being effective.

The other problem with this, is that every time you move your attention away from getting those emails done, or writing a book chapter, or listening to that conference call, you have to invest time and mental energy re-focusing on the task at hand. This is because you have to re-engage your attention, which takes much more effort than just keeping it on one thing in the first place. And every time you do that, you are actually becoming less effective and less efficient, because you are programming your brain to have a short attention span, making it so hard to learn to focus on one thing at a time again. Insert scream here!

Just like with energy and time, which are finite resources, so too is your attention, and it needs to be managed accordingly. We think that all the technologies, tools and gizmos help us to multi-task more effectively. Hopefully, you can see now, that it's just not true. So, so sad, I know.

Now before you go and do something desperate, to dull your depression at this new revelation, hold tight. There is good news. You can actually build your capacity to sustain your attention – yes, even up to a mammoth amount of time like a full 90 minutes (don't fall over, its true). It's like a muscle. The more you use it, the better you get at it.

···• Cultivating your attention

In terms of maximising your focus, there are some small things you can do to really help yourself out and build your attention muscle. The most effective technique that I know of, and that is supported by research for building and enhancing attention, is mindfulness practice and meditation. There is a lot on both in this book, and it is there for a reason, because of all the beautiful and transformative benefits they both offer for our lives. In Chapter 5, we looked at mindfulness practices, and why it is so important to learn to be here now; not everywhere and anywhere else our mind wants to take us. Practise the technique I outlined, and the meditations outlined in Chapter 25, and you will be helping train your mind to focus.

There are now also a range of computer-based programs and games that can be used on children and adults, to help build attention capability. Do a *Google* search and you will find them out there; try them out and see if they work for you. It's definitely worth a try. But for me, the mindfulness and meditation practices will always be the way to go – those monks who can sit on a cushion and stare at the wall for eight hours straight, coming out in a state of complete bliss, have to be doing something right. My money's on what they know.

Dial down distraction

Imagine how effective you would be if you could actually focus on the thing you were doing, and only on that. Wow, I just had to stop typing, so I could try to imagine it. I got it in the end! In order to really focus our attention on what we set out to do, here are some of the best picks from the research I have done about enabling your ability to focus, and getting the right things done.

- **Pick three** – each day, pick just three key things that you have to get done. Of course, there will be lots of other stuff that happens during your day. But by having three big things to do (and no more than three), you can stay centred and focused, and ensure you accomplish them. Let's call this your 'Most Important Stuff' list (MIS – sorry I couldn't think of a cooler acronym). These should be the things that are really high impact, and will make the biggest impact on your day/week/life.

- **Do them first** – don't do anything else in the morning until you have finished your MIS list. Okay, okay, you can go to the bathroom, brush your teeth, take a shower, get breakfast, drop the kids at school etc. Of course. I should have said, when you start work, don't do anything else, just your list. This means no email, no *Facebook*, no *Twitter*, no phone calls, nothing, unless it is one of your top three. We know that our brains focus much better first thing in the morning, when our self-regulation resources are strong and our brains are active after a night's sleep. So power through your list, without interruption, first thing.

- **Clear the path** – when you sit down to work, and you really intend to work, clear your path of all of the things that may distract you. You know what they are – turn off your email alerts, close all programs that you might be tempted to flick over to, you know, just to check what is happening (yeah right, before losing two hours). Yes, that would be your social networking sites, your personal email, blogs, and any other Internet connection that will pull your focus away. Shut it all down.

···• **While you're at it, clear your desk** – don't our desks just become the biggest dumping ground you have ever seen? God, I hope it's not just me. By the end of any given week, or even a hectic workday, my home office desk can look like a bomb has hit it. Papers, bills, pens, school newsletters, photos, books, forms to fill in, aromatherapy oils, Buddhas big and small, mala beads, inspiration cards, phone, Mac, water bottle, cup of tea, candle, crystals, incense, calendar, calculator, eye glass cleaner, (oh-my-god-save-me-now!). This is just some of what is on my desk as I write this. I know! And that is after I did a clean up today. Shocker. The more we have around us, the less focused we are, and the less energy will flow into our workspace, and our work. Don't worry; I'm doing another massive clean-up tomorrow, trust me. Join me and get rid of anything that doesn't need to be there.

···• **Give yourself good breaks** – we all need periods of time to just goof off, and our brains certainly do. So don't be unrealistic with the amount of time you are expecting yourself to stay focused. We need brain breaks. Give yourself a good chunk of time each day to just do nothing, to play, have some fun, do all that social networking and connecting you are longing for, and just waste time if you want to (yes, that's me). When you go back to work, to focus your attention, you will be much more primed to do so.

···• Is there such a thing as healthy distraction?

What a great question, clever you. Good news at last. Yes, there is healthy distraction. Our brains get tired when we focus all of the time, so alternating intense periods of focus with some periods of distraction (dare I say focused distraction?) can be good for our work. As with everything, we need to balance the two. But taking our minds off a complex problem or work period can let our brains relax for a while, and let our subconscious mind have a go at the problem in the background – got to love that! We can also get inspired through our distractions. I know that when the words aren't flowing, flicking over to look at my vision boards on *Pinterest*, or picking up one of the hundreds of books I have littered all over my study, can sometimes spark inspiration and get me flowing again.

The key is to put some limits around your distraction so it is working for you. Give yourself a ten-minute break after every 50-minute work period. Get up and make a cup of tea, go for a quick walk, do a yoga pose or a mini meditation. Just don't go and get on your *Facebook* page or check your emails, as they are time and energy robbers. Before you know it, you will have lost an hour (or three – yes, you know it happens). Just keep a lid on it and a check on yourself.

At the end of the day, we can implement all of the productivity techniques in the world to help us focus, like the things I have outlined in this chapter. And they all can help us, or I wouldn't have included them. But if we don't learn to manage our minds, our constantly available and biggest source of distraction, we will never fully focus or reach our full potential. And it can be done. Even though my workspace is often in complete disarray, I can still sit down sometimes to work, and get in such a state of flow that I don't see anything other than my keyboard and screen. At other times, I cannot write a single word until my desk is completely clear. You need to find what works for you, as there is no single answer that is right for everyone, and it may change from day to day.

As with everything in this book, I am simply offering up some learnings, thoughts and suggestions – it is up to you to decide what to take in, what ideas to play with, and to work out what to implement that will help you in your life.

Getting real – *remember*

···• Mastering your attention really is an art form. The mind is a complicated thing. There is a scientific, as well as a social reason, why it is so darned hard to stay focused.

···• Don't beat yourself up. This is the world most of us live in today – a world of constant interruptions, by someone else or by ourselves, and it is largely how we have been programmed. But we can change it if we choose to.

···• Practise mindfulness techniques, do your meditation practice and limit your distractions, and you will be on your way to have more focus in your days. And when all else fails, take a long, deep, calming breath, and refocus again.

CHAPTER 7

Set boundaries

*That woman speaks eighteen languages
and can't say no in any of them.*

– Dorothy Parker

oundaries. What are they, I hear you ask? It is a question I get asked so often: when I coach individuals, when I speak to hundreds of people, and all places in between. Not just what they are of course, as we are all pretty smart, we get the concept. More often it's how on earth do I actually create them, and when I do, how do I keep them in place? It is not a surprising question really is it? Between work, friends, exercise, study, kids (or if not kids, a boyfriend who can really be a big kid), family, the house, the car, not to mention the shopping, the shoes, and the general body maintenance, who has time for boundaries?

Well, that's just the point. We need to make time. Because having effective boundaries in place actually creates time, helps us manage our energy, and can keep us on the track towards being a cool calm success, not a hot crazy mess.

Anyone who knows me, or has heard me speak, will know that this is one of my all-time favourite topics. I think it is one of the most important things we can do for ourselves, on the road to becoming healthy, well-balanced, successful women, in this ever increasingly chaotic, technological and all-consuming world we live in. In fact,

I would go as far as to say that I think it is really, really hard to achieve those things, if we aren't good at managing our boundaries.

The reality is that knowing your boundaries is a key part of respecting yourself, being able to state your needs, and letting people know what will and won't work for you. For our bosses, it helps to set expectations, so it is clear what you are and are not prepared to do. In our relationships, it helps to clarify what we need and what is and isn't acceptable. And for ourselves, it is critical so that we have parameters around our work, social and personal lives, so we can manage our careers, our families and our health and wellbeing.

When you don't establish and respect your boundaries, you are essentially saying that other people's needs are more important than your own. Now, that may not be your intention, and you may not even believe that. But when you say 'yes' when you know you should be saying 'no', this is the outcome. And the more you do it, the more you let those boundaries slip, the less your needs will be met. Sometimes this is necessary, when it's a need from your child, or an urgent, one-off requirement from your boss. But when these things become the norm instead of the exception, then we have a problem.

Many of us have trouble establishing boundaries. We can be unclear on what they should look like, worry that people won't accept them, worry you won't be able to implement them. So you think to hell with it; it's all just too hard. Then the question becomes, how badly do you want what you want? For many of us, the need to please has been so deeply ingrained in us from an early age, so switching our brains to 'me first' can be too much of a hurdle to jump over. But it can be done.

Mandy, a 35-year-old director of a multinational company, wanted a peaceful Christmas with her husband, while staying with his family over the holidays. They always stayed with his family, even though her family was only 20 minutes away. She always felt compromised and resentful that she didn't get enough time with her family and friends, let alone time by herself to recharge from her busy job and life. Put simply, her needs were not being met, which was no surprise, as she had never clearly articulated them. She had not yet found her voice, and was unclear what her boundaries should be in this scenario, in order to make herself happy.

In one of our coaching sessions, we worked out what her needs were. They were pretty simple in fact, and she was actually quite clear about what she wanted when she thought about it. She wanted to be able to spend time with her parents without feeling guilty that she wasn't with her husband; she wanted a night out with her girlfriends during their week-long stay; she wanted to go out for a walk on her own if she felt she needed some space from his big family; and she didn't want to feel guilty about any of it. These were not unreasonable requests.

Through our sessions, Mandy discovered that she needed to calmly and clearly state her needs to her husband, and set boundaries around these needs; whereas before she had just silently fumed when the holiday had not gone how she wanted (for about five years, I might add). By doing this, she respected herself, and set the expectation of what her holiday needed to look like with the boundaries she set. She was delighted that, when she shared this with her husband, he was supportive and understanding, and all went well for their holiday together.

So what can you do to become better at knowing, setting and managing boundaries for yourself? Let's break this down to make it easier to gain clarity.

···• Knowing your boundaries

The first step is to understand what your boundaries should look like. This is all about what your needs are, and not at all about pleasing everyone else. Let me repeat. This is about you. What you need. It's about what will make your work life or home life (or both) more effective, enjoyable and manageable. Now many women I know find this really hard. And I have, too, in the past. We are used to servicing everyone else's needs before our own, and when we look at this differently it can be quite confronting. That's okay. It's a process that can take time.

We start by identifying the areas where we need some boundaries. Think about things like the time you leave the office each day or on certain days of the week. Or about the boundaries you need to set in your relationship about domestic work at home (we could write a whole book on this one); or the boundaries you need to place about looking after your health. I find that these are three of the primary areas many women focus on first.

The work one is huge, as the parameters we set here determine so much of how our life works. For me, when I changed my life six years ago, I set up my next role to be four days a week. I set very clear boundaries around my day off (Friday) and I was very clear with my boss, my peers, my team and my assistant regarding Friday, as well as parameters for my other working days. While this took a while for me to implement, knowing what I needed (picking up my son from school two days a week, not taking calls on Fridays, although I would check my email etc.) allowed me to manage my working week effectively and maintain my sanity. And I chose the role carefully, as I knew I could manage my boundaries effectively, whereas in some other roles this would not have been possible at all. So there needs to be a reality check there too.

···• Setting your boundaries

Once you have identified what boundaries you want to set for yourself, effectively communicating with the key people they impact is critical. You can get into trouble really fast, if you have decided to leave the office at 4pm twice a week, but have not communicated this with your boss, in an environment where this discussion would be expected. Not a good strategy. Similarly, setting a boundary of not doing the washing up one night (your agreed chore), taking a bubble bath instead, but not communicating this to your partner or setting a new expectation with him (or her), can also create a potential issue.

When you set new boundaries, things change. Your expectations of yourself, your expectations of others, and importantly, the way others view you and what you are doing, are all key factors that need to be managed. This does not need to be hard, but it does need to happen. Otherwise you are running your own race, all on your own, and people will get left behind. And they may not like it. So identify what your boundaries are, set them, and discuss and communicate with people who are impacted, so you can clearly articulate what you are doing, why, and what support you need from those in your life. You will find the process so much easier when you do this. And the change will have a much greater chance of sticking.

···• **Managing your boundaries**

Now comes the potentially challenging part. It's one thing to work out what boundaries you want to set, and another to tell people – but it's a whole other story to manage and enforce them, when the rubber hits the road. And the cold hard truth of it is that you are the only one who can manage them. Yep, you're gonna have to do it. But it can be done.

Years ago, my friend Michelle used to work for me. Not only was she the most productive person I ever had in my team, she was also the best at managing herself and the boundaries she had set up. She was exceptionally clear about how she wanted to work, how she performed at her best, and most importantly, at executing her personal and professional life to honour the boundaries she had set for herself. She still astounds me with what she can accomplish, and a large part of it is how she manages her boundaries.

The hardest part about all of this is keeping your boundaries in place when you're in the thick of it, and people are crossing them, pushing back on them, or just flat out ignoring them. Now, as we know, we live in the real world. From time to time, you may need to make an allowance and one of your boundaries may slip a little. And that may be okay from time to time. But here's the thing. If you continually let this happen, your boundary turns into a blurred dotted line, and eventually it can become all too easy to just give up altogether. Boundaries need to be kept in check. You are the only one who can do it, and you are worth the effort.

Getting real – *remember*

···• Take a look at your professional and personal life, and work out where you need to create some boundaries. If you don't know where to start, think about the times when you feel compromised, resentful or uncomfortable at work or home – this will be a good sign of where your boundaries may have been crossed.

···• Take the time and thoughtful effort to determine how to implement new boundaries. Then clearly communicate them to those around you, so they have clear expectations of what you will and won't do, when you can do it, what is acceptable, and what isn't.

···• You matter. It can be challenging to go down this path. However, it is essential if you want to be a strong, successful, well woman who is respected by others, and by yourself.

CHAPTER 8

Know your non-negotiables

The most courageous act is still to think for yourself. Aloud.

– Coco Chanel

I n the previous chapter, we covered boundary setting, and you could probably tell how passionate I am about that topic. Now we get on to something that is equally important, and sits right by the bedside of boundaries: non-negotiables. Non-negotiables are exactly that – things in your life that you are not prepared to negotiate on. They define not only what you will and won't accept from others, say a boss or a partner, but they also define what you will and won't accept from yourself. They are the deal breakers. They are unique to you and your situation, only you can determine what they are, and only you can manage them.

Non-negotiables can be anything. There are tons of examples, but here are just a few to get your thoughts started:

···• not working on weekends as it's family time

···• having Thursday nights to yourself for your study program

···• your weekly massage

···• going for a run each day

···• getting up at 5.30am to meditate

···• taking five weeks leave every year

···• picking your child up from school

···• being in bed by 11pm

···• the amount of project work you will take on at any one time

···• not taking work calls, or checking your *Blackberry* after a set time

···• your husband/boyfriend not leaving his dirty clothes on the bedroom floor (or leaving the toilet seat up, or any other domestic bliss robber that just kills you)

···• only working four days a week, and not working on your day off

You get the drift. Some of these may seem huge, some may seem relatively minor, but they are highly individual. So what may seem small to one person, can be life-changing to the person standing next to you. It doesn't matter what other people think about your non-negotiables. It only matters what they mean to you.

Here are some of mine. I only have a small list, but the ones on the list are carved in stone:

···• **Being an active, engaged, present parent** – absolutely my number one. Whether this is picking up Luca from school, being involved in school programs, taking time to read and meditate together at night, Saturday sport or family vacations, this is critical for me. I judge everything I am asked to get involved with, by how it helps or hinders me in achieving this.

···• **Managing my health and wellbeing** – this is absolutely non-negotiable to me. I recall years ago when I was still struggling with my health, and particularly my eating patterns, a friend said to me: 'I will not compromise my health for anything.' That really stuck with me, as I used to compromise my health for everything – work, my routine, my studies or family responsibilities. It took me a long time to make my health and wellbeing non-negotiable. Quality sleep, nutritious food, meditation and yoga time, and not overloading myself are all key aspects of this, all of which we will get into in Part Three.

···• **My work schedule** – in my current corporate work, I won't work more than four days a week on a regular basis. My fifth day is reserved for my writing, yoga, wellness work, domestic stuff, a fun afternoon with Luca and a little down time. This day makes me feel like I can manage whatever happens on Monday through Thursday, regardless of how busy I am, because then, there is Friday. Even though I am still busy on that day, it has a different energy to it.

We need to be able to determine the things that are real non-negotiables, from the things that are just good to haves, but are not really deal breakers. Checking in with your values, and your life vision, are good ways to validate what your non-negotiables really are. You might like to go for a run every day, but realise that four days a week is really fine, and the extra three days are just 'nice to haves'. They are not deal breakers. But missing those four days – out of the question. Similarly, you might like to leave the office at 5pm everyday, but as long as you get out the door on time three days a week, you are still content. Having this clarity is really important, so you don't get yourself in a state over something that wasn't even a deal breaker to start with.

Getting real – *remember*

···• Get clear – identify what your non-negotiables are, write them down, and ensure you have clarity between them and the 'nice to haves' in your life.

···• Keep it current – as your life changes, so does what is important for you in order to live your life in a way that works and is meaningful. Review your list a few times a year, to make sure your non-negotiables still resonate.

···• Get aligned – as with your values, if you continually have your needs unfulfilled, you will find it difficult, if not impossible, to live a happy, balanced, successful life. Align your life so that your non-negotiables are clear, respected and met.

CHAPTER 9

Be respectful, kind and grateful

Rain your kindness equally on all.

– Buddha

This chapter might seem like pretty basic advice. You know, it's almost like saying 'be good to your mother.' Well, of course. But hold the phone for just a minute. There is a lot more to this, than just that. While showing respect, being kind and being grateful might seem like basic manners (which of course they are), they are also scientifically-studied ways for inducing positive emotions and making us happier, increasing our wellbeing and improving our overall life satisfaction. Got your attention now? Let's take a closer look.

···· Be respectful

We all know those people who are really nice to you when they want something, but couldn't be bothered to give you the time of day any other time. Or the person who kisses up to the boss, but is a royal pain in the ass to her team, when no-one is looking. Or the person who couldn't be bothered to look or care, if the cleaner or office mail boy was falling down the stairs. You know who I'm talking about. These people have little or no respect for other people; particularly those who cannot help them get ahead.

Being respectful is core to being the best version of you. Everyone matters. Everyone. I don't care who they are, what job they are doing, what they look like, what clothes they are wearing, if they work three levels up or three levels down from you, or even if they continually walk in late to meetings and eat with their mouth open during them (yep, pet hate that one). Everyone is important.

Now this doesn't mean you need to like everyone. Completely different. I certainly don't like everyone that I come into contact with, but I do try to treat everyone with respect just the same (although it's trying at times, I will admit). And it also pays to remember, when we are speaking of respect, that you never know what people are dealing with, and sometimes a little respect goes a long way. I was in a meeting with a team member the other week, and thought she seemed a bit off – she wasn't as clear and on top of things as she usually is. I resisted the urge to criticise or ask why she hadn't delivered what she said she would in time for the meeting, respecting that she must have a reason why. She had to rush off the call and I didn't get a chance to check on her, so I called one of the other team members to see if she was all right. Turned out that one of her friends had committed suicide the day before. Shocking and totally devastating. Of course she wasn't in a position to be on top of things, and it was a miracle she was even on the call in the first place. You just don't know what people are dealing with, so be respectful and walk with grace whenever possible. Oh, and note to self – this goes for yourself too: don't forget to treat yourself with the respect you deserve. More on that coming up in Part Three.

···• Be kind

We all know what it means to be kind and we know that it makes us feel good, useful, needed and alive. It makes us feel good, because being kind triggers a number of physical and psychological responses, which are often referred to as the 'helpers high'. When you do something kind, your body gives you a little reward by releasing endorphins – morphine-like substances that give you the feel-good juice, and that can even reduce the feeling of pain. Get me some of those guys!

One of the greatest ways to be kind is by being altruistic. We all know it's something we should do. Help those less fortunate. Help an old lady across the street. Give to charity. Do something purely for someone else's benefit, with no expectation of anything in return. But more than just something nice to do, acts of altruism have been scientifically proven to increase your happiness and wellbeing. But here is the thing – you have to do this purely for altruistic reasons, because if you are only doing it to look good or to have someone thank you, then you're not really being altruistic. Sorry to burst your kindness bubble before you even start.

But relax – you don't need to perform grand acts to get the feel-good kicker. Small, simple, random acts of kindness will do just fine. Giving someone a smile as you walk down the street, picking up someone's papers that they have dropped in the office, putting a dollar in someone's expiring parking meter – these are all random acts, seemingly small, but with big pay-offs – for you and for the receiver. So build your kindness muscle, and not only will you make someone else's day, but you will be happier and healthier for your efforts.

···• Be grateful

It's pretty easy to go through our days bemoaning the things that happen to us, big and small. Whether your coffee is too cold or takes too long to be made; you can't find your favourite top to wear to work; your car won't start; or your boss is being a royal pain in the ass, it is all too easy to get caught up in the little things that make us complain and feel sorry for ourselves.

Gratitude, on the other hand, is a completely different emotion, and puts us in a very different state of mind. As I sit writing this, I am looking out a huge window at frozen Lake Louise in Canada, watching ice skaters spinning around the ice. My son is sitting next to me watching a movie on his Mac, and I am really grateful for where I am, having my family close by, and having the time and energy to write today. Now, I have a sore back, a bit of a headache, I am pretty tired from jet lag and a little hungry. But I am not choosing to focus on those things. I am focusing on being really grateful for the good stuff around me right now.

Gratitude is an emotional state, and it's an attitude. It can drive greater life satisfaction when we induce it, when we take the time to feel grateful and appreciative, and when we express those feelings to ourselves, or others. When we do this, life seems to improve, the small things seem to matter less, and we have a greater level of contentment and happiness. Expressing gratitude, not surprisingly, can also significantly improve our relationships, which also makes us happier. And it's all proven by science. Nice one.

So, how can you bring a state of gratitude into your life more frequently? You can start by looking at your day-to-day life and thinking of the many things that you are grateful for. Is it the peace of your morning routine, your evening run, having time to talk to a friend on your way to work, getting a coffee with work colleagues before your first meeting, walking your son to school, having a great meeting with your boss, that fresh salad you had for lunch (and gratitude for making the healthy choice, good on you), taking time to meditate at the end of your day, reading time before bed, watching your favourite TV show, playing with your kids, your partner saving the last piece of chocolate cake for you, or maybe taking time to have a lavender bubble bath. The list is literally endless. Gratitude can be for small things; it can be for big things. It can be expressed for people, or it can be experienced in quiet personal moments. The important thing is to induce it whenever possible.

Respect. Kindness. Gratitude. Seemingly small things, that we sometimes take for granted, but that have such a significant impact on the quality of our own lives and of those around us. So take some time today to be mindful of these things. Think about how you can bring more of them into your daily life, and notice how you feel when you do. You will also lead by example, and show others how you wish to be treated, by bestowing these behavioural gifts on others. Lovely.

Getting real – *try this*

···• Respect – watch your thoughts, words and behaviours for a few days and see how respectful you actually are, to yourself and to others. Think about how you can bring more respect into your life and change any negative patterns that may come up for you.

···• Kindness – write down three different acts of kindness you can perform, and find opportunities every week to do them. They don't have to be big, and can be as small as giving a smile to a stranger. Get creative – you might just have fun.

···• Gratitude – what were you grateful for today? Every night, before you go to bed, write down three good things that happened to you that day. Keep this as your gratitude journal, and watch your perspective change. It is also proven that this helps you sleep better – a nice little added bonus.

CHAPTER 10

Create positive change

If you don't like something, change it. If you can't change it, change your attitude.

– Maya Angelou

Aristotle said that *we are what we repeatedly do*. He also said that *excellence is therefore not an act, but a habit*. In Part Three, we will look at creating positive rituals. In this chapter, to set that up, I want to look at the process of change. In my life, really understanding how to change something, especially a bad habit, has been one of my greatest struggles. I have known many times what I wanted to change, but didn't have the knowledge I needed to implement it. Perhaps you can relate. You start a new diet on a Monday and wonder why, as an intelligent, self-motivated, driven person, you cannot seem to keep the cupcake out of your mouth by Wednesday. What's up with that? Or you wonder why you can't seem to kick your procrastination habit, your lack of exercise habit, your bad work habit or any other part of your existence that is not serving you well. Sound familiar at all?

Understanding the process of change, why we are the way we are, and how to change when you really want to, is all incredibly important. In Part One of this book we are focusing on strong personal attributes. I believe that the attribute of driving effective change can give you the keys to the kingdom of your success and happiness. However, it can keep you in the deep dark hole of frustration, that can lead to self-defeat and low self-esteem, if you don't learn how to use it. One of my goals for this book is to empower you to create the career and life you want. Knowing how to create change, and to create positive habits for yourself, is a critical part of this equation.

So let's start with what we typically know. We know that changing behaviours is hard. Change is hard, period. We get wired to certain patterns of behaviour, and our brains especially get stuck in a groove that takes concerted, conscious and consistent effort to change. And even when we do manage to change for a few days, weeks or months, it is all too easy to slip back into our old patterns.

The good news is that we know, through the latest neuroscience, that our brains are 'plastic'. This means they can create new neural pathways (like brain train tracks), which allow us to create change and form new patterns of behaviour that over time, can stick. We find our new groove, so to speak. But it takes work. Sometimes, it takes a lot of work. And it takes time. The popular myth that you can quickly and easily change a deeply-ingrained habit in 21 days has been largely disproven by brain and behavioural scientists in recent years. They now think that it actually takes anywhere from six to nine months to create the new neural pathways that support changing behaviour – hmmm, no more of those quick fix plans for me – or for you either. Sorry.

In her fabulous book, *This Year I Will … How to Finally Change a Habit, Keep a Resolution, or Make a Dream Come True*, MJ Ryan tells us that there are three things needed to make any change, whether it is mental, emotional or physical: desire, intent and persistence. Our pop culture society is filled with women's magazine covers that tell us we can meet our dream partner by the weekend, land our dream job in five days, or lose ten kilos in two weeks. This can leave the mere mortals among us feeling completely inadequate when we fail to do these things, which are completely unrealistic, if not downright impossible, to get done in the first place.

So what does it really take to make a successful, lasting, enduring change in our lives? First, we need to understand the cycle of change.

···• The change cycle

Two researchers and authors, James Prochaska and Carlo Diclemente, have developed and written about their change methodology, in *The Wheel of Change*. Their research has found that people cycle through five specific stages on any change journey.

We start with **pre-contemplation.** This is the stage when you really aren't aware that you want to change anything – it's the 'Problem? Who has a problem?' stage. It may sound familiar. There is no point trying to force someone in this stage to change something, as they really aren't conscious of it at all.

The second stage is **contemplation.** This is where you have awareness that a certain behaviour is troublesome, and you are seriously considering making a change. However, you are still at the stage where the change ahead seems huge, and the effort to change is much greater than the pain of staying the same, so it is not uncommon for nothing to really happen. You know how it goes – your skinny jeans look so good sitting in the corner, but you really aren't ready to put the chocolate away just yet, so you bury them under a pile of clothes, so you won't have to look at them. That's okay, you are still contemplating, and you're just not ready yet.

The third stage is **preparation.** This is where you are really serious about making a change, and you are starting to make plans to take action. You're ready to start, good for you!

Action is the next stage, and this is where the work really starts. This stage requires time and energy – yep, you are going to have to actually work for it. This is when you will change your behaviour, to overcome the problem.

And finally, we get to the **maintenance** stage (thank God), which could last from six months to an extended period, where you are bedding down the changes in behaviour you have implemented in the action stage, and reinforcing those neural pathways that you have created along the change timeline.

It is not uncommon to cycle through the change stages multiple times when changing a behaviour. This is completely normal and still productive, as each time you cycle through you pick up new skills and adaptable behaviours, that will support you in making the change stick. Trust me, I have been there and done that. But persistence pays off, and if you keep at it, you will be successful. You just have to want it badly enough – more on that in a moment.

So, if you are in the contemplation or the preparation phase of the change cycle, what are the things you need to know, and what do you have to focus on to ensure success? Well, I am so pleased you asked. Let's take a look.

···· Making change happen
In *This Year I Will*, MJ Ryan tells us that the top ten resolution pitfalls look something like this:

1. being vague about what you want
2. not making a serious commitment
3. procrastinating and excuse making
4. being unwilling to go through the awkward phase
5. not setting up a tracking and reminder system
6. expecting perfection; falling into guilt, shame, regret
7. trying to go it alone
8. telling yourself self-limiting rut stories
9. not having backup plans
10. turning slip-ups into give-ups

When you consider that only eight percent of people actually follow through their resolutions to a successful outcome, you can see that most of us fall into one, or many, of the traps above. The key is to understand enough about the change process, and yourself, to smooth a path to success.

So what are the steps and considerations? Here are some questions to think about, as you begin to create positive change in a lasting way:

···• *You really to have to want it*

There is no point in saying you are going to stop working so much, so you can get some semblance of balance in your life, if in reality you really don't care that much about balance, and you really love to work. Who are you doing it for? Don't kid yourself. You must be serious and care about the change you decide to make, so you are willing to work for it and follow through.

···• *What need is being served by what you are doing now?*

Your current behaviour is there for a reason, or you wouldn't be doing it. Hard to swallow, but true. Whether you're a workaholic, 20 kilos overweight, have anger management issues, or are unhappily single – your current situation is serving you somehow. So take some time to think about this. Whether the need is relaxation but the behaviour is binge drinking; or the need is recognition but the behaviour is overwork to prove yourself; you first need to identify what need is being served by your current behaviour. Once you have the answer, you can work out how to meet this need in another way, smoothing the path to change.

···• *How else can you meet your needs?*

So, you have identified the current behaviour and how it is serving you – that's fantastic. Now I want you to think about how else you could get this same need met. For me, eating cupcakes, chocolate or other things, that I downright know are not only bad for me, but proven to leave me feeling tired, grumpy and full of self-loathing, is less about the food, and more about the nurturing, comfort, or distraction they are providing for me, particularly when I am feeling tired or overwhelmed by all I have on. I also know, that retreating to my meditation cushion, my yoga mat, the bath tub, or even my bed, will give me a much greater sense of the nurturing I need, without the guilt, crash in self-esteem for not following through on my intention, and of course, the kilos (oh my skinny jeans, how I long for you). So when you think about the needs you have, how else can they be met?

···• *What's the price of not changing?*

You will experience ambivalence on the change path, no question about it. That's okay. But to progress down the road, you have to ask yourself, *what is the price of not changing?* If you really want a promotion, but are too fearful to ask for the management development training that you need, the price is staying in the same role. Is overcoming your fear worth the goal? Or if you really want to get healthy, lose weight and get fit, but you don't want to have to cut the sugar and get out walking, what is the price of that behaviour? Putting on yet another ten kilos? Think about and write down any negative effects your current behaviours are creating in your life – self-loathing, boredom, career stagnation, frustration. Once you have hit this wall of realisation, you are in the perfect place to turn around and move forward.

···• *What positive image can pull you forward?*

We know, from research in the fields of positive psychology and neuroscience, that we have more success when we are moving towards something positive, than moving away from something negative. And we know that positive images pull us forward. Think vision boards, athletes visualising their performance success, or thinking through the positive outcome of a business presentation before it takes place. It works, and science now proves that it does. So what positive image of the outcome you want can you visualise, to pull you towards success? Come up with one, have it firmly in your mind, place it on a wall, in your computer, in your journal, or anywhere you will reference it, and look at it frequently. It can be especially helpful when your resolve is slipping, to remind you what you are working so hard for.

···· *Are you acknowledging success?*

When we have made progress on our change efforts, it is really important to acknowledge that achievement. When we celebrate our efforts, we create upward spirals of momentum, that help reinforce the positive change and make it stick. Recognising your efforts also helps to reinforce the direction you are moving, and motivates you further towards your goals. We will cover this in detail in Chapter 14, *Create your goals*. But for now, just know that recognising, acknowledging and celebrating your progress, however small, are keys to success on your change path.

Change can be challenging. Anyone who has tried to change a habit knows this is true. But it is possible. And you can smooth the path to success by being aware of the cycle of change, being prepared, and being consistent. The result is worth the effort, if you want it badly enough to work for it.

Getting real – *remember*

···• Make sure you want it – don't kid yourself about wanting to change something that you really don't care about, and don't try and change for anyone else. If it doesn't matter to you, you will be wasting your time, energy and effort. You have to make sure you want the change, and that you want it for you.

···• Be prepared – trying to change a habit or pattern of behaviour without doing the required preparation is a path to failure. Do your homework; know what is going to be required, and get your ducks lined up. This will have a significantly positive impact on your process, how you feel about it, and your chances of success.

···• Keep going – if you want it badly enough, then you will still want it, even if you slip up. Don't be too hard on yourself, and hold the change process lightly. If you are persistent and consistent, it will happen.

CHAPTER 11

Get happy

Happiness is something that comes into our lives
through doors we don't even remember leaving open.

– Rose Lane

In this chapter, we are going to look at how to get happy. Yep, we are, so brace yourself, especially those skeptics among you. And we are not just talking about that fleeting happy feeling we get, when we do something great at work, or have a special moment with our child or partner, or buy that fabulous sparkly pair of new shoes (hard to beat I know). What we are going to talk about is the relatively new science of happiness. Don't worry, I am not going to bore you with a whole spate of scientific ramblings – there are great books out there (heaps of them) that do that. What I do want to do, is shed a little light on what we have learnt in the past decade about getting happy, staying happy, and helping those around us to do the same.

So what are we talking about when we talk about happiness? What we are really after is that sense of wellbeing that makes us feel like all is right with the world. And who doesn't want that? Well, I would say that just about everyone wants it, whether they can articulate it or not. But how do we get it, and is it available to everyone? Let's take a little look at what the science tells us, and then get into some practical, do-it-for-yourself tricks and tips, that will get you glowing from the inside out.

Let's start with what we know. Researchers have been investigating the science of happiness for well over a decade. Martin Seligman, father of positive psychology, decided back in 1998 that the psychology profession should start looking at what is right with people, and what makes us flourish, rather than just trying to get people back to a baseline from depression or other disorders. Pretty smart guy. The good news is that, while some people are born with a happier disposition than others, change is possible for everyone. We all have what is called a happiness set range – think of it like the healthy weight range – and we can influence where we sit within this range. In their book *Happiness,* Ed Diener and Robert Biswas-Diener tell us that there are new habits we can form, behaviours we can change, and choices we can make, that all have an impact on how happy we are. They talk about psychological wealth as the experience of wellbeing and high quality of life. We are not just talking about a fleeting high, as I talked about earlier. This is deeper – we have this wealth when we feel that our life is excellent. In their book, Ed and Robert list the following elements as essential components of psychological wealth:

···• life satisfaction and happiness
···• spirituality and meaning in life
···• positive attitudes and emotions
···• loving social relationships
···• engaging activities and work
···• values and life goals to achieve them
···• physical and mental health
···• material sufficiency to meet our needs

It's an interesting list and, not surprisingly, we are covering these key areas throughout this book – pretty cool, right? But there is a still a small potential glitch. While everyone arguably wants to be happier, some people don't want to make the changes necessary to become that way.

So why should you bother? Well, it's pretty simple really. We know that people who are happier get so much more out of life – they are more productive at work, get better jobs and like what they do more than their unhappy counterparts. They do better in school, great for all of our kids, many of whom are now being taught happiness practices in the classroom; they are more deeply involved in being of service to others; they have better relationships, including romantic ones; they have better health and live longer; they are more creative; and they are more likely to make time for leisure, hobbies and learning new skills.

On the work front, Shawn Achor, author of *The Happiness Advantage*, also tells us: *Data abounds showing that happy workers have higher levels of productivity, produce higher sales, perform better in leadership positions, and receive higher performance ratings and higher pay. They also enjoy more job security and are less likely to take sick days, to quit, or to become burned out.*

Okay, I think we have the 'why bother' question sorted, right? Great. So, let's look at how we get more of the happy juice in our days.

···• How do you boost your happiness?

Now, if you are still thinking *well that's fine for **those** people, you know, the ones who were born happier or have a perfect life*, hold your fire. You can influence how happy you are, if you are willing to make some different choices and do a little work. Because we all have a happiness set range and we can influence where we sit in that range, we need to look at our daily lives and see how each of these things is impacting on our happiness – for better or for worse. We will look at the scientific stuff that we know boosts our happiness levels in a minute. But first, have a think about which circumstances and behaviours make your day and life just that little bit sweeter.

For me, circumstances that make me happier include spending time with Luca like we did today – hanging at home all morning, going down to the skate park so he could scoot around with some mates, and then relaxing at home for the rest of the day. Having a job that I love and working with people I really enjoy is also a key one, as is having the opportunity to write this book about a topic I am so passionate about. As far as behaviours go, I know that when I am being kind and nourishing toward myself, through doing my yoga and meditation practice, eating healthy food and preparing it for others, getting enough sleep and going for a walk on the beach, I am so much happier than when I am not practising these behaviours. So these are all happiness boosters for me. What's on your list?

···· What do all those smart professors reckon?

So here is the good news (and you will hopefully see how clever I am). Throughout this book, I cover many of the scientifically-proven ways to boost your happiness. Told you I had you covered! Expressing gratitude, exercise, being kind and altruistic, nurturing relationships, using your strengths, and practising meditation are all covered in this book, and are all booster shots for your happiness. I'm so loving that. There are also a few other things that are both proven and recommended that will add to your life when applied. So let's look at them, and then you will have the full list and can get started.

···· *Keep a journal*

Whether you want to write mammoth pages in a notebook about every detail of your life, or keep a scrapbook filled with pictures from magazines and words in crayon, there are a multitude of ways to keep a journal. I do a mixture of both, and have done so ever since I was a little girl; although these days it is more pictures than words that I am drawn to. Journaling contributes to our happiness, by giving us a safe place to express our emotions, and enlightening our hope about the future.

···· *Savour the moment*

This should come as no surprise. When we take time to appreciate the positive experiences we have in our lives, we are savouring the moment. I have talked about celebrating success, in the chapter on creating positive change. Too often, we just rush straight on to the next experience, and we don't take the time to enjoy what has just happened. We rush on to dessert without savouring our main meal; we get straight on to the next project without celebrating the success of the one we just finished; or we don't stop to celebrate a massive achievement like completing a university degree or getting a big promotion at work (that would be me by the way, all of the above). We need to learn to stop, recall and savour the moment. It has a profound effect on our happiness when we do.

···• *Don't hold a grudge*

Again, this isn't rocket science. You know how you feel when you are holding on to some anger, frustration or resentment. It feels pretty bloody awful, right? You bet it does. We know why we do it. We want to feel vindicated, so we keep playing the incident over and over in our minds, whether it be a big thing, or a small incident. While we can do that, and stay mad, it doesn't serve anyone. And researchers have shown that the thoughts and behaviours linked to forgiveness do produce happiness. It can't be forced, you really have to feel it, and it can't be rushed. Sometimes it can take time, even a lot of time. That's okay. The important thing is to make the decision to forgive, and to let go. When you are ready, think about doing something that signifies your decision, like writing a letter forgiving the person who has wronged you. You can send it, but you don't even need to. Just feel it, write it, and then burn it. You will have completed the forgiveness ritual, and you can move on.

···• *Choose your mindset*

It will likely come as no surprise that some people have a mindset that enables them to be happy more often, and some people don't. Carol Dweck, world-renowned psychologist and professor at Stanford

University, has discovered a phenomenon called growth and fixed mindset. People who have a growth mindset believe in change, and they have the ability to continually improve and develop. They therefore work on self-improvement, learning and challenging themselves. They are people with a 'can-do' attitude, who never stop working on themselves and striving for improvement. People with a fixed mindset, on the other hand, think that their intelligence and performance ability is fixed, and not open for improvement. They therefore don't challenge themselves, as they have a failure mentality. Now it will also come as no surprise that growth mindset leads to more success, and it leads to more happiness. You can change your mindset, which is good news for those reading who think they are 'fixed'. Check out Carol's book *Mindset, a New Psychology of Success* – you can see my website for all the details. In the meantime, start to notice your assumptions and challenge your thoughts, when you think you can't do something. You will be on your way to challenging any fixed thoughts you may have.

We all want to be happy. Science now tells us that we can influence our happiness, and that there is a path to follow that will get us there. Throughout this book, we will cover many of the known ways to get your happiness on. You might like to come back to this chapter, once you have read the rest of the book, as you will then have many of the tools you need to make it happen for you, and for those around you. And remember what Ann Brashares said in the delightful movie *The Sisterhood of the Travelling Pants*: *Being happy isn't having everything in your life be perfect. Maybe it's about stringing together all the little things.* So true. So don't forget the little things either.

Getting real – *remember*

···• We all have a happiness set range, and we can influence where we sit in this range, by what we do every day.

···• Our circumstances and our behaviours influence how happy we are. And they are largely in your control.

···• Look at your happiness boosters – what can you do to gear your day toward things that you know make you happier? Which of the additional scientific things can you add to your day, to set yourself up for success and happiness? Think about it, plan some activities, and implement them. Your smile will thank you for it.

Creating a Career You Love

Go confidently in the direction of your dreams.
Live the life you've imagined.

– Thoreau

Wow, it's time for Part Two already? *Awesome.* (Can you tell how much I love this stuff?) In this section, we are focusing on your career. But not just any career – I want us to focus on creating a career that you will love. Work that you will be busting to get at every day, that you are purposeful about, where you are kicking goals and fulfilling your dreams. Sounds good, right?

The saying goes: *we are here for a good time, not a long time* (not sure who said it but it sounds about right). Part of that good time, for me anyway, has to be about meaningful, enjoyable, light-my-fire work. Work that taps into my passions, aligns with my values, uses my strengths and all that other great stuff we covered in Part One. This is where you get to see how that all comes together in a meaningful way, to support your career, and to help you live your dreams.

In this part of the book, we will absolutely get in touch with what your purpose is. Maybe you already know this and you are on the right path; maybe you need time and space to stop and re-evaluate it. You will get the chance here. We will check out those dreams of yours, and look at how you are travelling towards making them happen. We will get into your goals, your personal brand (yep, get ready for that). We will look at getting the basics right and getting the right things done. And we will focus on a few of the other biggies – relationships and emotions at work. And then, just in case you needed a little bit extra, I'll throw in some leadership thinking and give you some help with making the right moves and choices – just for the cherry on top.

That's a lot to get through – we better get to it! Let's go.

CHAPTER 12

Find your purpose

*Here is a test to find whether your mission on
earth is finished: if you're alive, it isn't.*

– Richard Bach

When you are feeling most alive in your work, what are you doing? When you feel useful, who are you helping? What work could you do that you would never want to stop, that you would never quit talking about, and that you would do without earning a single cent? Answer those questions and you will get a glimpse (or a massive big lightning bolt message) of what your purpose is.

I have a page from an *Oprah* magazine stuck on the wall above my desk at home, on my vision wall. It is a piece Oprah wrote, on finding your purpose. It resonated with me because, at the time, I was struggling to articulate what my purpose was. I was enjoying what I was doing for work, and I was studying wellness; I was coaching, and dabbling in some new areas. But I had no idea how they would all come together, or if they would at all. I couldn't yet see the big picture, as it was still evolving. The pull out quote from the article says: *Once you clarify your purpose for doing something, the way to do it becomes clear.*

They were powerful words for me, because they got me thinking about the 'why'. Why was I so passionate about all of the things

I was doing? Why was I studying and implementing all of these things – yoga, meditation, wellness, positive psychology, change management, leadership and culture? Why was I so happy, content and alive when I was doing these things? When I sat down and got quiet and clear, I realised that my purpose, my *why*, was to help people and organisations create positive change. That was it. And Oprah was right (no surprise) – once I got clear on this, the way to fulfill this purpose became as clear as crystal.

In this section of the book, we are talking about your career – how to build a career that you absolutely love. Work that you cannot wait to get to every day; that you leap out of bed for, filled with anticipation and excitement for all that your day will bring. That is my wish for you, and I hope that some of the words in this book will ignite that spark, or stoke the fire of purpose that may already be burning within you. So let's look at the *why* and *how* of finding your purposeful path.

···· Why be purposeful?

Other than the obvious reason – you know, you get to love your work – there are many other reasons why being on purpose is so important; and they mostly revolve around yep, you guessed it, loving your life. So let's talk about the whole work life thing for a minute (yes we have to, but it won't take long). I really don't like the term work-life-balance. I know I am not alone (and yes, you can throw up all over it now, if you want to). It has become one of the most loathed phrases around, and is often greeted with scepticism. Work-life-balance. It's not the balance part I have an issue with. I believe in balance. Some don't buy it, and that's okay. But I think that to be happy, contented and well, we need to have balance in our lives. It is what the sages from the ages have taught us. Balance the Yin with the Yang. Yes, I believe in that and try to live it – it has become one of the keys to my happiness.

But it's the work-life part I take major issue with. What that says to me is that we have to balance the work – you know, the part we have to do (and the inference being we don't like it) – with the life part – the rest of the time that we get to enjoy ourselves. Really? Is that how we want to experience the joy of life? That may have been a truism back in the 1920s, when work was in a factory on a conveyer belt for eight hours a day, punching in and punching out, before finally getting to clock off and go home to relax.

But we are not in that world anymore. And we have choices. If we are living on purpose, then we love our work; our work ignites our spark and fuels our passion; and doesn't really feel like work at all. We don't need to separate our work and our life. We need to integrate them, so that we can achieve balance with all of the elements of how we live, and do it happily. And we need to find our purpose. We want to love what we do every day with every fibre of our being.

So, that is why purpose is important. Phew, I am glad I got that off my chest!

···· So, where are you?

So, let's start with where you are. How do you currently view your work? Do you view it as a job, something you have to front up to every day to pay the bills? Where is your focus? Is it on acquiring skills, gaining power and self-esteem, and crawling your way up the ladder? Or is there a chance you see your work as a calling, something you are compelled to do because of your internal drive and motivation; because it makes you come alive, fills you up with passion and creativity, and you believe it is good for the world?

When I think of being on purpose career-wise, this is what I think of. I think of people I admire for their work, people who seem to have it all going on – are they just working to make a living, or is it bigger than that? I think of people like Oprah – it is so clear that Oprah is living a life of purpose – her work is her calling and it is her gift to the world. It would be amazing if we could all have that for ourselves.

···• Choose your own path

You don't need to be Oprah to have a purpose. And it doesn't need to be grand. It just needs to be you. Authentically you. When you are on purpose, you are on your own path. But getting your feet on the right path can sometimes be harder than you think. When we are tied up in our busy-ness – working hard to make money, pay the bills, or get ahead – we can so easily get lost on a road that looks nothing like what we thought it would, and doesn't lead to where we thought it would either. You know it doesn't feel quite right. You know it's not tapping into your passion, as we talked about in Chapter 1. You know you aren't using your strengths, or working in a way that is aligned to your values, and it's just not lighting your fire as it could be.

But when you don't listen to that thing we call intuition – your gut, your inner knowing – it is really easy to just keep going, push the discomfort down (way, way down) and ignore the fact that you are not on purpose. That you are walking on someone else's path. That you are not being authentic to who you are, and what you really truly want to be doing with your career (and, oh yes, that small thing called your *life*).

So, who decides which path you are on? Who decides if you are working and living on purpose or not? Lean in and I will share the secret – *you do*. You knew that, right? It's your choice. So choose. I know you can. Will you?

···• Staying the course

Once you find your purpose, you need to stay the course. While writing this book, I got to the stage where I had to tune out of what others had written before me. I literally had to stop reading books. I had to put the blinkers on. Otherwise I felt I would be swayed by someone else's voice, other's opinions, other's views. And as a writer, writing this book, I have my own. I have all of the above. And I couldn't question myself, or measure the worth of my words, by the barometer of what others had written before me (and drive myself crazy in the process). I just had to trust and believe enough in my purpose, my message and my voice, to write it all down. And so I put the blinkers on, like the horses on the racetrack. I kept in my lane, and followed my path.

You have to find your success on your own terms. Stay true to your plan, to your purpose. I can look around at people who are doing amazing things. This is especially poignant for me when I see fabulous, smart, inspiring people publishing books on topics that I am passionate about, thinking about or writing about. But I have to remind myself to stay on my own path. Stay true to my message. Bring my gifts forward for the world and not get sidetracked or swayed by what others are doing. And most importantly, not get disheartened that someone else has done it first, said it first, or written it before me. It has all been said before anyway, right? It is only our voice and message that resonates differently. I am on my purposeful path. *My purposeful path*. And so are you, if you choose to be.

···• Finding your purpose

For a practical approach to finding your purpose, we turn to one of my favourite professors. Tal Ben Shahar is the best-selling author of *Happier* and the infamous Prof who ran the most popular course at Harvard (on positive psychology – you know, teaching people how to be happy – go figure). He has a great exercise to help you find your purposeful path. Tal says that *you can identify your calling, by looking at the intersection between your strengths and where you find meaning and pleasure.*

Think about what is meaningful to you, what provides you with that sense of purpose you are seeking. Think about what you enjoy doing, where you find pleasure. Then go back and revisit your strengths that we looked at in Chapter 4, and recall what you are good at. Now here is the cool part. Where you see the overlap – you know, the things that use your strengths, are pleasurable and meaningful for you – this is your calling, your purpose. The trick is to find out how you can get to this sweet spot in your work. Have a go at this and see what you come up with.

If you are still struggling to uncover what your purposeful work might look like, or you want to take the soulful approach, be still for a few moments and think about this. What did you want to do with your life, before you were told what to do? Before you decided that there was a path you were 'meant to' follow. Before the world rained down a hailstorm on your dreams and told you 'no'. No. Oh, how I hate that word. And how dare they. What did that picture look like? If you can get quiet enough and think back to who you were then, and what you dreamt about, you may tap into something that was purposeful for you. What might that look like? Can you find it? I know you can. Will you?

When we are working and living with purpose, we are alive, so very alive. So take some time with this one, before you move on. Then get real about what this means for you, so that you can work on purpose, light your fire, ignite your spark, and get your glow and flow on every day of your life. How exciting would that be? Dwell in the possibility of that for a few moments, and then, begin.

Getting real – *remember*

···• When you are working on purpose, you have a burning desire to do what you do. If you're not feeling that fire, it's time for a rethink.

···• Ask yourself the question: Is this moving me further down my purposeful path? (This is one of my favourites by the way.) If you can answer a big 'yes' (or even a hell yeah), you are on purpose, so keep going. If your answer is 'no', then look at your motivation for what you are doing.

···• Stay the course. It is your career, and you have a unique purpose to fulfil. Don't get swayed by looking at what others are doing, and compare yourself to their progress. The only path that matters is the one you are on. Stay true.

CHAPTER 13

Dream big, then do the work

*It's the possibility of having a dream come
true that makes life interesting.*

– Paulo Coelho, *The Alchemist*

So I had some major news this week. I found out that I landed a publishing contract with Hay House for this very book you are reading. Wow, I hear you say. You bet – beyond excited! I have been floating on a cloud all week, trying to savour the moment, while at the same time trying to get grounded in the reality of it all, as my head has been literally in the clouds.

And then a funny thing happened in the car today, that helped me put my feet back on the ground. It was the usual Saturday morning run around with Luca, driving out to the boogie board store to change some flippers (that actually didn't need changing), and then off to the Apple store to get a backup machine for my Mac (even though we never ended up getting there). You get the drift. But during this endless driving around in the pouring rain, I said to my son, 'you know, I can't believe that I actually have a publishing contract, and with my dream publisher'. And he looked at me with a seriousness and tone that belied his 11 years and said, 'believe it Mum, you really are making all of your dreams come true, and you've worked really hard for it.' I was floored by his insight. And he was right. He has always been an old soul, but that is for another story.

Dreams. It's a big word, and a scary topic for some. And it's a long-buried one for others. How many people had big dreams growing up, or at one point in their lives, only to be lost in the chaos that becomes life, and buried under the pressure and routine that can become daily existence. I know I have been there in the past, more than once.

When I was growing up, I only had one dream from age of about three until 24 – become a movie star. The plan was to move to Hollywood after drama school, and be a famous actress, with homes in three countries and married to Charlie Sheen by age 25 (well, at least I dodged *that* bullet). When I hit 25 and the dream had not eventuated, and I was on my way to changing paths, I was devastated. My 25th birthday was so utterly miserable, frustrating for all those around me, who could not understand what I could not articulate – that I was heartbroken.

When I look back now, I had the dream, the big dream, but I didn't really do the work. Yes, I spent my teenage years on the stage, and yes, I went to drama coaching, drama school, speech lessons, performed in the theatre and took endless dance classes. And yes, I really did have some talent. But I never really had the self-esteem or confidence to take it to the next level. Nor did I have the sponsors and support network to help me believe I could make it. For so many reasons, I never pursued it to the point where success could blossom. And then at 24, fate stepped in and I had a car accident, which caused me to pause, and to change my path. And then, in time, I created a new dream, and built a new path.

Lao Tzu said: *Water your dreams with optimism and solutions and you will cultivate success.* It is really important to have the dream, whatever that may be. The big job, the dreamy man (or woman), the fancy house, family, travel, dream career. You need to know what your dream is, define it as best you can, visualise it, write it down and set goals around it. And then you need to do the work that will see you attain it. We can believe in *The Secret* all we want, and yes, I believe you can manifest your destiny (you should see my vision wall), but you also have to do the work. As I like to say, *hope is not a strategy,* you need more than that to get to where you want to be.

So what does 'the work' look like? Let me give you an example that is close to my heart, and very timely. For about a decade now, I've had this desire to write a book for women. I have been writing ever since I was a little girl, whether it was poems, stories or, in my angst-ridden teens, songs about despair and all those teenage emotions (remember them?). I had a deep knowing, somewhere long hidden, that this was my path – to be a writer. And so I spent lots of time, on and off over the years, planning, doodling, jotting down ideas, discussing concepts, tossing ideas around and writing draft pieces. I knew that the books would flow, when I made the decision to do it. And all that doodling and dreaming helped me to incubate my vision, until it was ready to be let out in the open. And then the real work began. For me, the work in writing this book and securing my publishing contract looked something like this:

···• ***Define the dream*** – The picture of the dream, this book, has morphed many times, but it has always been based around sharing my message with the world, to empower and inspire women. As one of my soul sisters, Taren, told me during the week, I have been manifesting and working on this very book for about a decade, it didn't just pop out of left field.

···• ***Get clarity*** – While a book has been floating around for ages, I had to get clarity on which book I was going to write. Clarity on message and book content. Clarity on mode of publishing. Self-publishing is fabulous these days; but for me, I always envisioned signing with a major publishing house, with global distribution and Hay House was my ultimate destination. I was clear on that, and it became my goal.

···• **Visualise success** – On my inspiration wall at home, I wrote the following on a card: *I am a best-selling author, published with Hay House. I am an amazing success and love everything about it.* Above that on another card, I wrote: *The New York Times Bestseller – 'A Memo to My Generation' – Megan Dalla-Camina.* I look at this every day, and had to smile to myself the day I got signed to Hay House, when sitting at my desk looking at my wall (just so you know, *A Memo* was the original working title).

···• **Do the work** – The work involved the writing, and it still does. I wrote even when I didn't know what I was writing, for whom, or for what purpose. I researched writers, writing, publishing, agents, and went to The Writer's Workshop that led to me joining Hay House. Months went into writing the best book proposal I could muster. And then submitting it, detaching from the outcome, and continuing to pursue the path. Oh, and of course, there was writing the actual book. Hours and days and nights – when the sun was shining in the middle of summer on a Sunday afternoon and I wanted to be at the beach – but I sat at my desk and I wrote. You have to do the work, no matter how badly you would like to be doing something else.

Dreams are great. They can be the guiding light on our paths, that keep us hanging in there when nothing else does. They can be the thing that galvanises us into action, helping us break through obstacles and achieve the impossible. But we have to remember to do the work.

We hear all the time that you have to work *hard*. Hard is such an awful word; it actually feels painful to me. And work was like that for me for a long time. But I no longer believe that work has to be hard; I just believe that it has to happen. We can work with grace and ease, and it can be a magical experience. Writing this book was an absolute pleasure. I'd get butterflies in my stomach when sitting down to put my thoughts on paper, or researching a chapter to share some inspiration with you. But it also took many, many hours of dedicated work, and many things were given up in the process (yep, I missed my beach and Saturday nights with my girlfriends for many months). But it was worth it, and I hope you agree as you read this, and think about your own dreams.

I think that the ultimate test of a dream is how badly we want it, and what we are prepared to do to get it. Because I truly believe, and tell my son whenever he will listen, that no matter how big or crazy your dream is, if you are prepared to do the work, anything and everything is possible. And in the next chapter, we will look at creating step-by-step goals to help you get there.

Getting real – *remember*

···• Get clear on your dreams and take the reality test – how badly do you really want them and what are you prepared to do to get them?

···• I read a quote once that said if you want to have what others don't, you have to do what others won't. What is the work you are going to do to make your dreams come true?

···• Don't let others deter you from what you really want, and are prepared to work for. They are your dreams, it's your work, and that is all that matters. Dream big. Believe it. Make it happen.

CHAPTER 14

Create your goals

Goals are dreams with deadlines.

– Diana Scharf Hunt

S o you have discovered your purpose, chosen your path and dreamt a huge big tantalising dream of what your amazingly bright career is going to look like. Phew, must be time for a nap! Sorry, not just yet, we have only just begun (is that Karen Carpenter I hear?). Now it's time for the work to kick in. It's fabulous to do the visioning, and incredibly important that you do. It's also incredibly important, critical in fact, that you set goals for yourself that see you moving forward on your career path, in the right direction, and at the right pace, to lead to the success you are dreaming about.

In Chapter 10, I outlined the process of creating positive change. We talked about the process of change, what the steps look like, and what some of the critical questions are throughout the process. In this chapter, we will look at the truth and rigour around effective goal setting.

Having clear goals not only gives us a sense of purpose and direction, they have also been shown to increase our overall life satisfaction and wellbeing. While we all want that, I am sure, setting and actually achieving concrete goals can be one the hardest things to do. I know this from my own journey, and I am sure you'd have some colourful stories of your own. We all have remnants of new year resolutions that lasted about, oh, let's say, five minutes. Sound familiar? Or we have that poignant moment on our birthday, especially those big scary round number birthdays, where we really, really, (really!) commit to setting a goal and believe we will actually follow through on it. But most times, we just don't get there.

So why persevere? Goals can make us feel hopeful for the future. When we have a goal to work towards, we feel like anything is possible, we feel good about ourselves. The momentum builds upon itself and spills over into other areas of our life in a positive way. It is no surprise either – it's actually science. *Hope Theory* founder, Rick Snyder, says that *when we have goals, we actually begin to think more creatively, as we look at ways to achieve them.* What he calls *pathways thinking* leads us to have a more hopeful outlook on life in general. We also know, from his research, that people who are hopeful are happier people, and they work more flexibly and persistently towards achieving what they want. More reasons to get those goals going now.

In this part of the book, we are looking at building the career you want and love. Setting career goals are important, as they give us something to move towards. Now I'm not saying that you need to have a career plan made out of cement, that is immovable, unshakeable and not up for negotiation. You have to be able to go with the flow to a certain extent, take opportunities when they arise, build new skills as they become needed, and take on projects that may lead you in a different direction. Of course. But what you don't want is to be so directionless that any opportunity looks like a good one, or that any role your boss wants you to do is a good idea; or you may just end up in a place in ten years that looks foreign, unfamiliar, and maybe really disappointing to you.

I have a journal with a quote on the front from Gary Lew that says: *this is your world, shape it or someone else will.* It is so true. Going through the stages you have already in this section of the book, and setting clear goals, will ensure you don't end up in a career desert land.

···· So what do you do?

Most of us grew up on SMART goals, and our kids are still taught them in school. You know what they are, right? SMART goals are specific, measurable, attainable, realistic and time bound. While SMART is a good framework for goal setting, researchers and scientists in the field of motivation have, in the past few years, discovered that there are also some other elements at play in successful goal attainment.

Gary Latham and Edwin Locke are the leading experts in goal setting theory, and co-authors of the book *A Theory in Goal Setting and Task Performance*. One of their key findings is, that if you are working towards a performance-based goal that you can easily measure (like getting a promotion, an A on a test, or losing four kilos), then instead of being realistic, your goal actually needs to be challenging.

Now this is something I have always believed. Why set a goal that is realistic, when you could stretch yourself to greater limits? I never saw the point. If it is realistic, then you really don't need to strive too far to get it, and usually end up underachieving. This is now proven by science. Thank you professors.

When you are looking at setting goals, the initial challenging goal may seem completely unattainable and more like a dream than a goal. But when you break it down into bite-sized chunks, you can actually see that it may be achievable after all.

Take this book for example. I had a goal to write this book, get an agent or a publisher for it, and have it in bookstores within a 12-month period. Now, most sane people, and certainly most of my writer friends, thought I was crazy, that this was completely unachievable. I was relayed a long list of reasons why this was impossible – most books take more than a year to write, not three months; you will need to submit your proposal to more than 20 (or 100) publishers before someone picks it up, if at all; you will never get an agent; and, particularly, I was told it would not happen because I also had a big job, other projects and a child to raise as a single mother. So how could I possibly find the time to write 70,000 words?

Now, they are all reasonable arguments, sure. If I were setting a realistic goal, I would have given myself a year to write the book, six to twelve months to get a publisher, and another year to have it in bookstores. But I have never been much of a realist, as you probably know by now. I set a challenging and specific goal, I broke it down into bite-sized chunks that I could manage, and what do you know, I have achieved it. The proof is you are holding it in your hot little hands right now (and hopefully loving it!).

So a goal needs to be challenging. Latham and Locke also agree with the specific part of SMART. They agree that goals need to be time bound, and they need to be measurable, to produce optimal results. So make sure you have a barometer of what success looks like, both along the way and at the end, so you are sure you know when you get there.

A couple of final points on goal setting, and then you can spend some time getting stuck in to it. The research tells us that we are more successful when we are moving towards something we want, rather than away from something we don't want. For those theory buffs among you, this is called *Approach versus Avoidance*. So, if you are looking to make a career move, you are better off to set a goal that says *have landed a promotion as marketing director by April 1st*, rather than *not still be in the same position at Easter*. You are moving towards a positive image, which we also know, pulls us forward to success (like the pictures of Jennifer Aniston on my vision wall – motivating me to get my butt out for a run!).

We also know that setting a goal that is rewarding to us personally, one that is intrinsically motivating and driven by our own interests and desires, is much more successful than having to work towards a goal that is extrinsically set by someone else, which is never as motivating. Of course, that makes sense.

My last point is to write it down. When I was growing up, whenever my Dad heard me talk about something I wanted – usually something like *become a famous movie star* – he always told me to write it down. Always. I have those words stamped in my brain and tattooed on my forehead (seriously, you will see them when we meet). I used to roll my eyes at him, as I am sure you can picture, little darling as I was growing up. And, of course, I never did it (hmmm, maybe that was the problem?). But we know categorically that when we write down what we want, in the form we have discussed in this chapter, we sign a contract with ourselves and we achieve superior results every time.

Oops, I lied (sorry) – one final, final point. Don't forget to celebrate success. We have already spoken about this in Chapter 10, so you know why it is so important in your life and career. It is especially important in goal setting and achievement. So whether celebration looks like champagne, a dinner out, buying your favourite magazine, a bubble bath, or a big reward like a holiday, make sure you are recognising and rewarding your achievements, both along the way and at the end of the path. You will spur yourself forwards when you savour the moment – you earned it and you deserve it – so celebrate it.

Getting real – *remember*

···• Take some time now to think about the career goals you want to set for yourself – is it a promotion, a lateral move, or a complete career change?

···• Work through the process of SMART, with the caveat of setting challenging goals. See what you come up with, and how you can break your ultimate goal into bite-sized chunks that are achievable.

···• Reward your success, and savour the moment when you get there. It will fuel you towards your next goal setting endeavour.

CHAPTER 15

Brand yourself fabulous

*Don't you ever let a soul in the world tell you
that you can't be exactly who you are.*

– Lady Gaga

P ersonal brand. Everyone has one. Many don't know what their personal brand says about them; and few do something positive to build it, enhance it, and leverage it to support their career success. I am still surprised by how many people think they don't even have one. Seriously. If you are alive and kicking, then you have a personal brand – even if you're in fifth grade.

We see, very visibly, the celebrity version of personal branding. Think Beyoncé, Madonna, or in recent times, the phenomenon that is Kim Kardashian. Whatever your opinion of her, she has turned the art of celebrity into a billion dollar business, almost entirely through the power of her personal brand.

So what does your brand say about you? What do you want it to say? Building a successful personal brand starts with knowing yourself. We have already covered passion, purpose, strengths and goals; so you are well on your way to really knowing who you are, what you want and where you are going. Hopefully you also agree that you have a personal brand, and need to nurture it to help you become the shining success you deserve to be. Fabulous. Now comes the tricky part – what to actually do.

When I was crafting the outline of this chapter, I noted down the first things that came to mind for me when I thought of 'Brand You' – and what some of the key contributing factors are. I think the list is worth sharing (only slightly edited), to warm you up and get you out of the traditional mindset *but I work so hard, isn't that enough?* Because building a successful personal brand (and career) is about a whole lot more than how many hours you put in at the office.

Now I warn you, some of these factors may be unpopular. But hold your judgment for a minute, and let's take a look:

···• how you look
···• what you wear
···• how you act
···• how you sound
···• your body language
···• your handshake
···• how you treat others
···• whether you are nice
···• whether you gossip
···• whether you are reliable
···• what you stand for
···• the roles you take
···• the roles you won't take
···• how hard you work
···• how hard people think you work
···• how often you speak up in meetings
···• how well you listen to others
···• who you know
···• your network
···• who knows you and talks about you
···• what they say
···• what you know

···• your reputation
···• who knows that you know what you know

Wow, it's a long list right! Well, that is just the start. At the end of the day, when it comes to your career, you are the product. Now that may sound deceptively simple, but how often do you think about yourself in that context? Be honest. So many people, women particularly, go to work, thinking that if they just work harder than anyone else (particularly their male colleagues) they will get ahead and get noticed. Sorry, but in so many cases it's just not true.

I cover many of the things in this list in other chapters, particularly in *Getting the basics right*, (Chapter 20); and really the bulk of this book contributes to creating your fabulous brand. So here I just want to cover a few key areas that are really important to think about, as you are building or refining your personal brand.

···• How you show up, and how others perceive you

Yes, yes, I know. I know you are going to completely shoot me down in flames for being so superficial, and talking about how you look at work. But I don't care. Well, I do care (of course) but I am going to tell you anyway, because it's really important. In fact, it's critical. How you look matters. How others perceive how you show up, matters.

Now, let's just clarify what I am not talking about. I am not talking about how thin you are, what designer clothes you wear, what colour your hair is, or whether you tote the latest and greatest handbag. I am also not talking about being corporate clones with chin-length bobs and the right suit and hose (that's pantyhose, not a garden hose, in case you were wondering). And I don't think we have to lose our authenticity and personal style, when we step into work. God forbid. It's not about any of that. What it is about is how you pull yourself together, the image that you give off to others, and the appropriateness of how you look for your workplace.

Now I hear some of you screaming at me through the pages, saying it should be all about the quality of the work, and not about how I look; that men don't get judged by what they wear; and that I should just be able to be myself at the office. Well, here are my answers to that – it isn't, they do, and you can. Right, glad we got that sorted! Let's keep it real here. You need to look professional. Whether you have on a $50 skirt, a $500 dollar skirt or anything in between, you have to look relevantly dressed for your workplace. If that is in an advertising agency or for a fashion magazine, then you may have some creative licence, more so than if you worked in a law firm (obviously). And if you are the boss you may have more licence again. But we also know that you should dress for the job you want, not the job you have, so keep that in mind too.

I once had a graduate rock up to a meeting with me, in what I could only describe as a see-through white blouse. Seriously, it was see-all-the-way-through. For a corporate environment (or anywhere really, other than a pole dancing club), that was completely inappropriate. What that said to me was that she was not aware of the environment she was working in, or she didn't take the time or care to dress in a way that was respectful of herself, or her colleagues. She was incredibly smart and capable, but she let herself down with her look and, like it or not, her intelligence was not what was being focused on.

I also had a senior manager in one of my teams, responsible for an important function, who came to work every day looking so dishevelled, that I wondered if she had slept in a barn. She really needed to put a brush through her hair, apply a little make-up and pull her outfit together. But she never did, even after much coaching, and she has not progressed upward in the organisation to this day.

You can say what you like and moan all you want – but appearance matters. It shows that you understand the rules, you respect the environment, you are a good representative of the company, and that you are worth investing in. So think about how you want to be perceived at work, and manage your image accordingly. Get a good haircut, look polished, clean your glasses, check your teeth after lunch, watch the jingle jangle jewellery factor, change your shoes when the heels are too scuffed to wear (just had to throw out a beloved pair after two years, as they were dead – devastated), and dress up for important meetings, even if it means you only have one really special suit or outfit. If you have a signature look, like always wearing bright coloured suits, or killer shoes, or a funky brooch on your jacket, go for it. It can become a key part of your brand and what you are known for. But keep the other points here in mind as you do. They may seem small and you may hate the fact that it matters, but it does. Look at the successful senior women around you, and you will see what I mean. And yes, it goes just the same for men, believe me (well, hopefully except for the bright coloured suits, but hey, if it works, work it!).

Oh, and on a final note, if you feel confined, constrained and you feel like you just don't fit with how you are expected to show up in your workplace, then here is a hint – you may be in the wrong job. So go back and think about your passion, purpose and all the other cool stuff we have already covered, and see where it leads you.

···· **What are you known for?**

Hopefully by now, you are getting an idea of who you are, or are crystallising your vision for who you want to be when you grow up (I want to be Donna Karan by the way, minus the fashion designing). To do that, of course you need to harness and build your skills and knowledge. And the key is to not only build them, but to become known for them, in a way that differentiates you from everyone else.

The days of being employed in one company and in one career went out the window in the eighties. Today, in the knowledge economy, it is all about talent. It is all about building eminence, thought leadership, unique skills that are in demand, and being known for what it is you can do that no one else can – or that you can do differently or better than anyone else. And critically, it is not just enough that you know what you know – others have to know that you know it.

Eminence is in the eye of the beholder. So, unless others recognise it in you, then you are really just an expert, all on your lonesome sitting in the corner, and where is the fun (or success) in that? So think about what you want to be known for, and how you can make that happen.

And remember – be specific. If you think you can be known for everything, you run the risk of being known for nothing at all. I know lots of stuff – business strategy, marketing, branding, change management, culture, leadership, positive psychology, coaching, wellness, yoga teaching, how to demolish a cupcake in three seconds – you get the drift. But what I want to be known for is what I am most passionate about – helping individuals and organisations to create positive change. So get clarity, build your deep expertise, and then you can make a big song and dance of it to others.

···• It's not just about looks and skills – it's also about behaviour

Many of things in my brainstorm list at the start of the chapter were not about knowledge, they weren't about how you looked, and they weren't about how firm your handshake is (but please ladies, this is not a time to be dainty) – they were about behaviours. I cannot stress this strongly enough, when you are thinking about branding yourself fabulous. What you are known for is as much about *how* you do what you do, as it is about *what* you actually do. In Chapter 20, we talk about 'getting the basics right', so check that out and master it. Because behaviours matter – big time.

···• Building and owning your personal brand online

Now of course, in this age of technical and connected everything, how you show up online is just as important (or maybe even more important) than how you show up to a meeting. How you represent yourself and your brand online can literally make or break you, in terms of others' perception, your reputation, and whether you are branding yourself fabulous, or just a little tragic.

Whether you are 25 or 55, if you are going to be online, then you need to be mindful of what you are saying, what others are saying about you, and how you manage both. And if you haven't done a *Google* search on yourself recently, then you need to do one, pronto! Knowing what is out there on the web when people are looking for you, whether it is a future employer, a client, or even a new boyfriend (here's hoping), is critical to managing your brand. So here are just a few considerations of your online brand aspects, and what to think about.

···• Blog and personal website

Firstly, go and buy your domain name.com. You don't want someone else registering your personal name domain, and trust me, it happens. At 25, this may not seem important. But by 35, when you change track and are making a name for yourself, it will matter, big time. If you have an area of expertise, and want to share what you know and create a dialogue, starting a blog is a great way of doing it. There is plenty of information out there on the web about how to be a great blogger, so I am not going to cover it here. But think about whether you have something new, different and interesting to blog about, then go do your research. It is a great asset to build your personal brand and thought leadership.

···• LinkedIn profile

As the 'go to' network for professionals, there is no better place to get connected online with people who may be able to help you further your career, make connections, and build your profile – and for you to help others. It is like your online, very well-publicised resume, and so much more. So invest good time and thought into how you want to be represented, and who you want to connect with, and then, go get linked in.

···• Facebook profile

Ah *Facebook*. How many careers have been damaged, job opportunities lost and reputations left in tatters, because of things posted on *Facebook*. I'd hate to count the numbers. *Facebook* is an amazing opportunity to network and build your connections, in a less formal way than *LinkedIn*. So if you want to use it for more than just connecting socially, go ahead. I connect with loads of people in a different and more intimate way on *Facebook*, and also with people who aren't on *LinkedIn*. So think about what your purpose is, before you go uploading your latest crazy photo of you and your favourite vodka bottle (I know you wouldn't, I know, but others have, and much, much worse). Think also about your *Twitter* profile and connections in the same way.

One final note on branding yourself fabulous: the best way you can build a strong and memorable personal brand is to help other people. The more you can reach out and help other people be successful, the more others will want to help you. There is little worse than someone who is blatant about self-promotion, and I see it all the time. It is off-putting, and I just want to get away as quickly as possible. If it takes me a few days (or longer) to return someone's call, they usually fall into this category. I know they just want to sell me something, ask a favour without one ever coming back to me, or just suck my time and energy through glorifying themselves. Don't be one of these people. Find out who you can help and how through your personal eminence, and you will find your sphere of influence and connection growing through doing the right thing. People want to help a helper, so be one.

Getting real – *remember*

···• You have a personal brand whether you like it or not. So better to take control and brand yourself fabulous, than to just stick your head in the sand (it's not good for the make-up anyway).

···• Think about how you look, how others perceive you, what you know and who knows it, and what your online profile says about you – you will have gone a long way to build the brand that works for you.

···• You need to self-promote, but don't gloat. Helping others first, through what you know and what you can do for them, is the best way to build endorsements that matter. And it all comes back to you in the end, so make sure it's the good stuff you are putting out there.

CHAPTER 16

Mind your emotions

If you haven't got anything nice to say about
anybody, come sit next to me.

– Alice Roosevelt Longworth

When we think about emotions at work, our minds usually go straight to *that* emotion – you know – *crying*. God forbid we should ever commit one of the all-time cardinal sins of the workplace, especially if we worked in PR maven Kelly Cutrone's New York office. Kelly is famous for saying: *if you have to cry, go outside* – she even wrote a book about it. Or think of Tom Hanks in that baseball movie *A League of Their Own* when Geena Davis starts crying – *Crying? There's no crying in baseball!* he exclaims, completely horrified. As I said, God forbid. Especially if you have a male boss (or a female boss who tries to act like a man – much, much worse).

But there is more to the discussion on emotions at work, than just shedding the odd tear or two. There has been a huge amount of research done in recent years about the benefits of emotion in the workplace, particularly around positive emotions. Back in time, if you saw someone enjoying himself or herself at work, you know, smiling at people, stopping for a friendly chat, and maybe even – wait for it – laughing, then they were obviously not serious about their work, and clearly didn't work very hard at all. But we now know, from the science of positive psychology and neuroscience, that eliciting positive emotions not only makes us happier at work, but it also makes us more productive, more creative, helps us think more laterally, and actually makes our brains work better to deliver better results.

If you want to be innovative at work, solve more problems, and build good relationships with colleagues and your boss, then you want to really look at this. Who ever thought you could achieve so much, just by kicking your happy genes into gear? Well you can, so let's look at the why, when and how of positive emotions – and what to do with the negative ones when they rear their ugly little heads.

···• The why of positive emotions

Groundbreaking psychologist, Barbara Fredrickson, has spent the past 20 years studying positive emotions, and the impact they have on people all over the world – pretty cool job. In a recent interview, she explains why we should up the ante on the positive. *When people increase their daily diets of positive emotions, they find more meaning and purpose in life. They also find that they receive more social support—or perhaps they just notice it more, because they're more attuned to the give-and-take between people. They report fewer aches and pains, headaches, and other physical symptoms. They show mindful awareness of the present moment and increased positive relations with others. They feel more effective at what they do. They're better able to savour the good things in life and can see more possible solutions to problems. And they sleep better.* Nice one.

Part of Barbara's research outlines the *Broaden-and-Build* theory, which is one of the cornerstones of positive psychology. This theory helps us to understand why it's so important to have the positive outweigh the negative in our day. In fact, her positivity ratio says that the minimum is three positive emotions to one negative emotion for happiness; but if you really want to thrive, you should be looking at anywhere up to six to one. And a note to all the parents out there – think about the interactions you have with your kids, and do a count of the positive to negative interactions – you could be surprised (or mildly horrified) at the reality. And the same goes for your relationship with your partner.

But I digress – back to *Broaden and Build*. This theory outlines that negative emotions, like fear and anger, lead to the brain actually narrowing its capacity and capability – like the lights being turned off – limiting our ability to think clearly, creatively and productively. On the other hand, positive emotions lead to cognitive flexibility, lighting up the neural pathways of our brains, broadening our abilities and, over time, building our resources like expanded skills and social ties.

I don't know about you, but I want some of that. But what exactly are positive emotions, and how do we get more of them in our days? Great questions. Let's take a look.

···• Cultivating the positive

To be able to cultivate positive emotions, we first need to know what they are, and we also need to be able to identify our feelings. In her book *Positivity*, Barbara Fredrickson explains the ten most common positive emotions. Remember, she has studied this her whole life, so this is no flighty research here – it's been going for a couple of decades. The top ten positive emotions are:

···• *Joy* – experienced from delightful and cherished experiences, where we feel light and vibrant.

···• *Gratitude* – we have talked about this already in Chapter 9, and it is experienced when we feel appreciation or are thankful for something or someone in our lives.

···• *Serenity* – a state of peacefulness and tranquility, experienced in those times when you can just be happy in the moment. I call it bliss.

.... *Interest* – comes when you are being curious, wondrous, or intrigued about the world around you. For me it comes through writing, study and reading. It's a big one for me.

.... *Hope* – the feeling that things will turn out for the best. I think this is one of the most critical, as without hope, what is there?

.... *Pride* – being able to feel dignified, accomplishing something that has a level of social value, and being proud about it. This can come from a sense of purpose and holding meaning in what you are doing.

.... *Amusement* – experiencing fun, humourous and playful situations, and being amused by others. Amusement helps us build connections with others too.

.... *Inspiration* – this comes when you have an uplifting or moving experience. This can happen when you see true goodness in someone. We can accomplish amazing things when we are inspired.

.... *Awe* – the feeling of wonder. Think about watching the ocean waves crash, admiring beautiful art, or looking at a structurally-amazing building. We think about how small we are, compared to the enormity of the world we live in.

.... *Love* – love is the grand prize, the compilation of all of the above. Love is about strong affection and personal attachment, strong positive feeling towards someone else. Love really is everything.

So there you have it. The ten scientifically-studied and researched positive emotions, that will lead you to the good life. How cool. So what do you do with it? The biggest part is to be aware of the emotions you are feeling, and choose to experience these positive ones whenever you can. Be open-minded, and allow for moments of joy, gratitude, inspiration and awe in your life. We are so busy, we don't often stop to think about how we are feeling, or if we are experiencing those moments of goodness that lead to happiness. Create the space and make the time, and watch the positivity flood in to your life.

Now, all of that goodness is not to say there isn't a role for negative emotions at work. We are not all Pollyanna here, by any means. The point with negative emotions, especially in the workplace, is to learn how to control them and to minimise any damage they may do.

Because they can do damage. We all have a colleague who flies off the handle at the smallest thing, leaving him branded difficult to deal with and hard to manage. Or the woman in sales who is a little frenetic, and you never quite know what is going to come at you, or when. Or the marketing manager who is so emotional, she has a temper tantrum one minute, cries the next, and is your best friend the minute after. None of these people are easy to deal with, and their behaviours are all career limiting to some degree. Not where you want to be.

So we have looked at how to enhance the positive emotions. How do we minimise the negative ones? Those nasties that turn up during your workday – what on earth is to be done about them? It's okay, I have you covered. Here are a few words to the wise.

···• Don't walk – run

Absolutely number one on the list for dealing with negative emotions at work, is to leave the situation and bide your time. Don't make decisions or have confrontations when you are angry, upset or just outright pissed off – don't worry, it happens to the best of us. We have all had times when our boss did something we thought was totally unprofessional, like undermining us in a meeting, or giving credit to someone else for our hard work. Yep, I have been there and wanted to absolutely strangle the guy (or just kick his ass – and you thought I was so nice). You may have had feelings of wanting to tell him (or her) what you really think of them, or just plain quit.

But you need to pause here, breathe and get a grip. Walking away, getting a coffee, sleeping on it, and getting some perspective, are all required in this situation. When we are in the throws of a downward spiral caused by negative emotions, our brain literally contracts. We cannot think clearly, as we know from looking at the *Broaden and Build* theory. So don't do anything rash or, I promise you, you will regret it later, when your brain (and hormones) have returned to their normal charming state. Time gives us perspective, and then you can deal with the situation in a calm and rational way.

···• Maintain your respect

We talked about respect in Chapter 9, and the upshot here is that you don't have to agree with the other person's position, to show respect for their emotional state. Now this is hard when there is really bad behaviour going on, and I would revert to walking away, if that is the case. But don't disparage the other person for having a different emotion from you; and try to be empathetic whenever possible.

···• Get to the why

Many times when we experience a negative emotion, it is because the situation or conversation has triggered something in us, and caused some form of resistance. If you try and ignore this emotion, it will keep rising up like a pimple that just won't go away (how rude). Sit with the emotion and get to the bottom of why this situation was such an issue for you – once you have calmed down of course, and have some space to do so. Try to get in touch with the root of the resistance, and you will help to distil the negative emotional response.

So there you have it. Minding your emotions at work is about a lot more than just learning not to cry in the office. Understanding the science and application of the positive, how to get more of it in your day, and what to do with the negative gremlins when they appear, are keys to the successful career you are working so hard to create. So think about it, get familiar with the positive emotions on the list, and look for as many opportunities as possible to elicit them in your day, and in others'. Your career will thank you for it.

Getting real – *try this*

···• Become aware of the present moment, because many moments are positive – you just aren't present to realise it. Be open to what is, and you will experience more of the positive emotions that are there all the time.

···• Do simple things to improve your mood, like getting outside in the sunshine. It's proven to give you a lift after just 30 minutes, so go get your rays on (with a hat, fab shades and sunscreen, of course).

···• Minimise your negative emotions by using your breath, meditation, and being mindful – check out the chapters on these topics, to increase your ability to focus on the positive, and live in the moment.

CHAPTER 17

It's all about relationships

Sometimes our light goes out, but is blown again into instant flame by an encounter with another human being.

– Albert Schweitzer

In his book *The Happiness Advantage,* Shawn Achor says that *social relationships are the single greatest invesment that people can make.*

He also shares a 70-year research study, one of the longest-running psychological studies of all time, where researchers investigated the life circumstances and personal characteristics that separated the happiest lives from the least successful ones. George Valliant, the director of this study for 40 years, says: *there are 70 years of evidence that our relationships with other people matter, and matter more than anything else in the world.* Pretty powerful stuff.

So how do your relationships at work shape up? Are they blooming, connected, mutually supportive, beneficial to your career, nurturing, and satisfying? How is your network? How aware and engaged are you in the office politics that fuel the show where you work? These are all really important questions. How you answer them can make a huge, career-shaping difference in your world (in case you missed it, this stuff is freakingly important).

So, where to begin? Well, let's look at each of these things in turn shall we? Let's see what you need to be thinking about and doing, to have rockin' relationships that will fuel your career success.

.... Okay, we know they matter – how do you build them?

I think the first rule of relationship building is getting to understand one really important point – it's not all about you (sorry). Jane Horan, author of *I Wish I'd Known That Earlier in My Career,* agrees. *Relationships begin with a genuine interest in people and having the ability to listen to the other's story. Everyone has a story to tell and by listening you gain tremendous insights and learn a lot.* Spot on. You are not going to build a very good or interesting relationship, if you can't connect with the other person on some level.

The fast track to connection is through listening and empathising. You have to be interested in the other person (or at least show interest, even if you aren't), be respectful, be helpful, show up and, really importantly as Jane highlights, you gotta listen. Relationships aren't a one-way street. You need to be present with another person and engage with them, to be able to build a connected relationship. Sounds easy, but so many people are not so great at the art of connection.

.... So now I have relationships – how do I build a network?

Oh, networking. For some reason, this still sounds like a dirty word to so many women. I hear all the time, *but Megan, I can't go to a pub after work and I don't play golf, so that kind of leaves me out of that networking stuff.* Well, if this was the eighties, I would probably agree with you. But the world has changed. Radically. And so has the science and art of building a network.

Jane Horan says: *Building a network depends on purpose, that is, are you trying to sell a new idea, drive change or build a career? Taking a deeper look at your network is important – determine who you would call for advice, who's the nay-sayer, who's always supportive and who's a critical thinker? Whether you're pitching a new idea or seeking career advice, this group can provide answers.*

Women are better at networking and do it more often than we think. And you don't have to go to a 'networking' breakfast or cocktail party to do it either. I rarely go to any formal events like this, but I have an extensive network. I have built this through my formal business connections, by seeking introductions, making connections through friends, and through reaching out to people I am interested in meeting via *LinkedIn, Facebook* or *Twitter* (my god, how did we do this before social media came in? I can't even remember).

Women are great at building and nurturing relationships. And we must nurture them, so they grow healthy and strong (and bear fruit, or pretty little blossoms!). There is little value in making a fabulous new business connection, only to let the contact dry up through lack of engagement. You need to, you know, *connect*. Drop people an email, with an article they may find of interest. Catch up for a coffee every quarter, to see what they are up to. Make regular posts on your social networking sites, so people know what you are doing business wise, and to keep things current. Nuture your network and watch it grow.

One last word on relationships and your network – think laterally about your connections. That father you speak to, at your kid's soccer match, could be your next boss. The fellow board member, at the non-profit you meet with once a quarter, could become your new mentor. And the woman you bump into, at your yoga class, could become your new business partner. Take the blinkers off and broaden your perspective on who you meet and how you can connect. You may just make some enlightening connections that amaze you.

···• **Navigating the politics**

We could not end a discussion on relationships at work, without talking about the big one – politics. Now usually that word is said with a sneer and a jibe, and has an aftermath of utter distaste. Jane has a different philosophy. *Too often the word politics is viewed negatively and frequently, it is ill-defined. Similar to networks and relationships, the first step is to embrace the political realities of organisational life. From a positive perspective, politics is all about relationships. From a negative perspective, politics surface issues of turf, silos, egos and hidden agendas. Savvy managers know how to embrace politics and understand the value in behind the scenes networking and ethical lobbying, to sell ideas or drive change.*

No matter where you work, politics will always be part of the equation – it's just a fact of doing business (and life – remember being a kid in the school yard? Same thing, different setting). Get your head around the dynamics of your workplace and your relationships, and you will be doing yourself a huge favour and setting yourself up for success.

So there you have it. Relationships. Arguably one of the most important topics in this entire book, when it comes to career success. One of the biggest career traps is to just focus on the work and think that will be enough. It's not. You have to make connections, build relationships, work your network, and know how to navigate the politics. As we have covered in many other areas of this book, head down and bum up will only get you so far. You have to be connected to get to where you want to go – and not forgetting where we started the chapter – be happy on your way there.

Getting real – *remember*

···• Relationships are everything. Remember to take as much time focusing on building lasting, fulfilling, connected relationships, as you do on honing your skills.

···• Relationships are the juice that makes our world and our work sing. Where you can, gravitate to those people who bring positive energy and make you feel uplifted, engaged and who help you to thrive. It's not always possible, as we can't always choose who we work with. But that's the good stuff you want more of, so seek it out.

···• Wonderful relationships are about giving. Actively listen. Be engaged. Be generous – with your time, your ideas, your connections, your knowledge. Offer help. Don't gossip. Be supportive. Be there when you are needed, and you will find that others will do the same for you.

CHAPTER 18

Role models, mentors and sponsors

We need role models who are going to break the mold.

– Carly Simon

They say it takes a village to raise a child, and I believe this to be true. I also believe it takes a network of people to create a successful career. We don't do it on our own; no matter how much we might like to believe we can. It's incredibly important in your career to have people around you who are your true supporters; to have people you can look up to; and to have those who you can take trusted advice from. So many women underestimate just how critical this is, not only for getting ahead, but also for building the self-confidence that will get you where you want to be. In this chapter, we look at three of the most important people you need in your career, why they have to be there, and what to do with them when you find them.

⸳⸳•• Role models

Role models are those people you look up to, admire, and who you may choose to emulate. They are inspirational figures in your life: people who pull you forward towards the version of your best self – the person you are working to become. You may know them well, you may not know them at all, or they may be a brief acquaintance who triggered something in you, that you wanted to seek out or develop in yourself.

I am writing this, having just come from dinner with my friend Naomi Wolf, feminist icon of my generation and social and political activist (yes I know, pretty lucky right?). I met Naomi through the SWB conference, when I was the Chairperson in 2007, and we have stayed in contact ever since. Naomi is one of my role models. She is someone I look up to for her integrity, her intellect, her passion for women and equality, her writing, and as I said to her this evening, for being the woman of character and consequence that I hope to be. In terms of an inspirational role model to pull you forwards, it doesn't get much more powerful than that, and I am most grateful.

Some of my other core role models include my parents: my father, for his dedication to his work, the respect he shows for others, and the relaxed, humorous take he has on life. My mother, for her grace and the unyielding way she loves her family and friends. My friend Michelle, for her scorching intellect, her supernatural effectiveness, and for her support as a friend. And there's my friend Taren, for her kind, loving nature, her passion and her ability to always see the best in people. I also have role models in my business life – people I admire for their personal attributes, the way they conduct business, or their business prowess.

And on the other end of the scale from those closest to me, are those who I don't know at all. The list is too long to note here, but it includes people like Oprah and Louise Hay, for the way they have changed the lives of millions of people, through their dedication to helping people live their best lives. Kris Carr, from *Crazy Sexy Life*, and Kimberly Snyder, for the way they inspire health and wellness in people all around the world. And then there are my guiding lights – Wayne Dyer, Deepak Chopra, Marianne Williamson and others – who nurture and uplift my spirit, and who inspire me to bring my gifts to the world in a way that is meaningful and that matters.

You get the picture. From each of these people, and many others, I watch, listen and I learn. I take on and emulate those behaviours and traits that resonate with my values, and that I believe will help me to become more of the person I choose to be.

Role models can inspire us and motivate us to keep moving forwards towards our goals. But there is one thing to remember. While you can admire others, look up to them, and choose to emulate parts of them, you still need to be true to your authentic self. I read a quote once, and I am not sure where it came from, that said, *don't judge your insides with anyone else's outsides*. I just love that. They are words to live by. Because no matter how much you admire someone, you never really know what is going on with that person, even those closest to you. So admire, respect, but always remain true to you.

···• **Mentors**

Most people understand the role of the mentor, but it never ceases to amaze me how few women, especially those who are actively trying to advance their careers, actually have one. Every time I speak to groups of women, I ask the question, *who has a mentor?* And I am usually stunned by how few hands go up.

Mentors are so important. A mentor is a person you turn to, when you have a question or need guidance in an area that they have experience you can draw on. Pretty simple. They are someone you can trust to advise you, think in your best interests, and steer you straight. You can reach out to different people for different purposes, and you can have many of them should you choose. Holly Ransom, one of my mentees who you met in the *Values* chapter, has a rigorous and thorough approach to building her mentoring network, which is well-established in her young and blossoming career.

I asked Holly recently about the needs that a mentor fulfils for her. She commented, *Wow, where to begin! For me, mentors have been the single biggest contributor to my growth and development as both a leader and a person – greater than any learning experience I've ever had within the four walls of a classroom. Developing a mentoring relationship provides me with the ability to continually undergo high-level learning, from the lifetimes of experience of people I have the utmost respect for, and who are absolute leaders in their field. They help me think through ways to tackle challenges, strategise and evaluate opportunities; they provide content specific advice in their areas of expertise; and they share their experiences and advice about their career, business, life and everything in between. Additionally, they push me to the heights they know I'm capable of, and they encourage and remind me of what I'm capable of, if I lose the ability to see it for myself.*

Holly has around ten mentors. This is a large number, however she has chosen them for specific needs she has: like one for non-profit work, one for strategy and another for managing her hectic life. You might have ten, or you might have one. The number isn't as important as being specific about what needs you have, and who in a mentoring role can help you fill them. Don't forget about chemistry either. While it's great to reach out to lots of different people as Holly has done, to gain a breadth and depth of mentoring advice, there has to be a connection between the two of you, or it doesn't work. A good mentoring relationship is organic and builds a life of its own, and it does this when there is a real chemistry between you. So keep tuned to your intuition when engaging, to ensure it's there and worth investing time in.

And remember, you need to give back and share the love as well. It's fabulous to have the opportunity to be mentored, and I personally am so grateful for those who have taken the time and energy to mentor me throughout my career. But I have also gotten so much benefit, personally and professionally, from those I have agreed to mentor, like Holly. It is an invaluable experience, and there are so many women out there who need your help, support, wisdom and guidance. So reach out to others and offer yourself – others will benefit, as will you.

···· **Sponsors**

When I speak on career topics to large rooms of women, especially gen X and gen Y women, a topic that is getting a lot of airtime recently is sponsors. Women generally feel that, if they just get on with the work and do a fabulous job, people will notice and it will be enough to get them the next great role, or the next promotion or project. But unfortunately, in today's workplace, it is just not enough (actually I don't think it ever has been). Keeping your head down and bum up, means that you often don't see what is going on around you, or who is talking to who. Before you know it, the guy next to you, who has a senior sponsor in the business, just got the promotion you have been busting your butt for. It happens every day. Now it's not the guy's fault. And it's not your fault either, as you haven't known any better. But you will now.

Sponsors are people in your career who are passionate advocates for you. It's like they wear a T-shirt with your name on it (not literally of course, but you get the gist). They may sponsor you into a new role, by lobbying for you in a way that can be more influential than other routes. They may make business introductions for you with key people you need to meet, to get you to your next position or opportunity. They may connect you with mentors, who can help you fill gaps in your skill base; or work on specific areas that you want to develop. And they can certainly help you navigate the politics of your organisation – and let's not forget how critical that is.

In terms of identifying sponsors, you should be able to easily point them out. They are the people who sing your praises whenever possible. They could be a current or former boss, someone you worked on a project with, or a former mentor. They could even be a former employee – you just don't know where people will end up in this interconnected, global world we now work in. And they don't even need to be more senior than you. So stretch your thinking and get outside the square. You may have more out there than you think.

Identify your sponsors and work out where they might be able to help you. There may be nothing at the moment, and that is fine. I can go for months without actively seeking out a request for help. But when you need it, reach out with a clear and respectful request for support, always acknowledging how grateful you are for their help (of course). In the meantime, nurture the relationship, and keep the connection alive and well.

Getting real – *try this*

···• Take some time to mindfully identify who your role models are and why. What is it about the person that you admire, and how can you bring a slice of that into your life, in an authentic way?

···• Do you have a mentor? What are you seeking mentoring on? Career skills, wellbeing, how to build your sales management expertise, how to create some balance in your life? You can seek out different mentors for different purposes, like Holly did. Sit down and make a list of the areas you need support in, and who could mentor you in that area. And if you don't know, ask your peer group, colleagues, boss or friends. People are usually happy to help when asked, so ask.

···• Work out who your sponsors are, and how and when you may be able to draw on their support. Do you have a career move coming up, that they could help you with? Is there a decision you need to make, that their perspective and guidance would be invaluable on? Nurture these relationships. You never know when you may need them.

CHAPTER 19

Lead from where you are

Give light and people will find the way.

– Ella Baker

Put your hand up, if you think that leadership is reserved for those in your organisations who are in a management position, and that it only applies to you if it is part of your job description? See, I knew you were so clever! Your hands are down, because you know so well that everyone is a leader, or can choose to be one, regardless of what role they are in today.

Leadership is not designated through a job. We see leaders everywhere. We see them in the café where you have your breakfast, in the mailroom in your office, in the classroom where your fifth grader is at school. Leaders are all around us. If you are breathing, you are a leader, or have the potential to be one, should you choose.

What we will focus on in this chapter are the qualities and behaviours of being a leader that you can instil, regardless of your current role, and the difference it will make not only to your career, but to your life. We all have the capacity for greatness. And the world, especially now, needs people from all corners to lead – to lead with integrity, compassion, possibility, clarity, kindness, purpose, humility and trust. What a wonderful world it would be, and we can help create it by how we show up, how we lead ourselves, and how we lead and inspire others.

So what does my version of leadership look like, and where did it come from? I have spent 20+ years working in organisations large and small (mostly huge), and I have seen leaders come in all shapes and sizes. And yes, I have experienced the good, the bad and the truly horrific. I have also spent a huge part of my career and my studies looking at what makes a great leader, and how people become one.

We are covering a huge amount of content in this book for you as an individual, but it also applies to your role as a leader. By the time you get through it, my hope is that you will have the tools you need to not only live an engaged, balanced and inspiring life, but you will be able to use those tools to engage and inspire others, by applying all of this wisdom to your role as a leader, in whatever capacity that may be for you.

So here, I am sharing my simple philosophies on leadership. I am not a perfect leader, in fact as you will have discovered, I am not perfect in anything – actually I don't even strive for perfection. What I strive for in my leadership, and what I want for you, is to care, to inspire, and to invoke greatness. Here are some thoughts I have for how to do just that.

···· Be clear on your mission

What is your role as a leader? What is your purpose? It doesn't matter where you sit in the team or in the organisation. It doesn't matter if you are at the top of the tree, the bottom, or floating around in the middle. It matters what your purpose is. It matters what you are setting out to accomplish, why you are doing it, who it will impact, for what end game, and what you intend to do to get it done. And it matters how you go about it too. There has been research done looking at hospital janitors, who see their purpose as critical in patient care. They are not just emptying buckets and mopping floors. They are helping to change and heal lives. They are working on their mission. And it makes the world of difference. Be clear on what your mission as a leader is, communicate it, get the support you need, and follow through. These are all key elements of great and transformational leadership, whatever your role.

···• Look for the best in people

A fundamental part of being a great leader is to lead with optimism and focus on people's strengths, instead of their weaknesses. We know from research that most managers focus on weaknesses – they look at what needs to be fixed. As we saw in the *Strengths* chapter, people flourish when we bring out their strengths. Compliment a team member on the way they handled a difficult negotiation, congratulate a peer on a great presentation, call a junior member of a colleagues team to say 'thank you' for organising that great sales event. Look for the best in people, find their strengths and acknowledge them. And watch people shine like diamonds.

···• Show people what's possible

Isn't the world so full of doom and gloom today? We are in arguably the worst global economic time of our generation, businesses are collapsing or just holding on, people are getting laid off, or are working harder than ever to keep their jobs. I could go on forever. But I choose not to. I choose to look for the possibilities around me. The possibilities at work for new and exciting projects, for where to drive the growth in the business, to mentor that new up-and-coming sales manager to help fulfil her potential, to help my son believe that he can achieve any goal he sets out to. They are all possibilities, and they are everywhere. We just need to shift the focus and find the right lenses. Help people create the space for possibility to be unveiled, and optimism will abound, even in the direst circumstances.

···• Have high expectations

People have a tendency to rise to the occasion. What does this mean? We know from psychology, that when a low bar is set, people will perhaps meet it, but not exceed it. It is not motivating or inspiring, and doesn't invoke great energy. When we set a high standard for someone to meet, whether it is a child in school, or a team member at work, they will strive to exceed it. Having low expectations for yourself, your work, your project peer team, or those you manage, doesn't do anybody any favours. Set high expectations, and then help people build the self-confidence and efficacy to achieve and exceed them. You can enable people to soar higher than they ever thought possible, by giving them the gift of believing that they can.

···· Do what's right, not what's easy

There is always an easy path. And then there is the right one. Great leaders, wherever they reside, choose the right one. And it is not always easy to do this. What is easy is to cut corners on a project; make the sale to the customer to make your sales plan, when you know they are not getting what they need; or tell the management team what they want to hear, instead of what they need to know. Leadership is about making the tough calls and following through with the tough actions when required. Great leaders do what's right, regardless of the consequences.

···· Tell the good stories, not the bad ones

One of the key tenets of good leadership is having great positive energy. Energy is infectious. Do you want people to be uplifted, inspired and motivated when they are around you, or do you want them to be demoralised, depressed and flat? Of course, you would choose the first option if you are sane (and we have already established that). But so many sane, well-intentioned people unthinkingly make a different choice by their actions, and particularly by their words and the stories they tell.

We don't want to be Pollyanna by any stretch, but where you can, tell the good stories. Tell the stories that will uplift and inspire people to strive for greatness, whatever level they are at. Tell stories of successes in the business, rather than the deals that didn't close or the project that failed. Tell the stories of great things you have seen people doing, rather than complaining of what isn't working. Energy is contagious, so make sure your contagion effect is a positive one.

···• Take the initiative

I once saw a new graduate in a business I worked in take the initiative soon after taking up her role (with about 100 other grads). She set up a networking group, that became the hub of the entire graduate program. Not an easy feat in a big organisation, and with little work experience. She was a leader, and she took the initiative to do something that she saw was an opportunity. Leaders take initiative. They don't wait to be asked or told what to do. They seek out opportunities, projects, things to fix, and ways to add value. And they make a difference.

···• Act as you want others to behave

Great leaders lead by example. This one is pretty simple really. If you want someone to act a certain way, whether it is a direct report, a teammate, a young graduate you are mentoring, or your child, one of the greatest ways to impact on their behaviour is to be an effective role model.

So how do great leaders behave? For me, they are enthusiastic, they are humble, they are open to the ideas of others, they speak with confidence and conviction, they help, they care about people, they are ethical, and they treat people with respect and kindness. You can come up with your own definition of what great leadership looks like. Define it, and then model it. If you want to be respected, respect others. If you want to be listened to, listen to others. If you want to be acknowledged, then acknowledge others. As I said, it is pretty simple.

···• Do great things

When I was working in marketing for a global professional services firm way back when, i was developing a new global brand for a new business – pretty exciting stuff. I travelled all over the world, spending heaps of time in New York and Tokyo, having meetings, creative sessions with advertising and branding agencies, and doing heaps of planning for the global launch. It was one of the best experiences of my career. One of the tag lines an agency came up with for the new campaign was 'Do Great Things'. I *loved* it. I completely fell in love with the concept, the campaign and everything about it. The reason it resonated so strongly with me, was because it was all about doing things that were amazing, interesting, and, well, great. It was inspirational and aspirational at the same time. Who doesn't want a life filled with great things, great work, great people, and great projects? Unfortunately, we never ran the campaign as the business never launched, but the thought always stayed with me. Gear your thinking and your work towards doing great things. You have to do stuff, so why not make it great? Think about that.

···• Leave a footprint

Leaders leave a footprint. What is the footprint you are leaving in your days, weeks, and years in your organisation? What does your team or peer group say about your work when you are not around? Do your projects matter? Are you influencing people in a positive way, that will make a difference in people's lives, and for the organisation? Some people are in roles for years, leave the group or the organisation, and it was like they were never there. Others can be in a team for three weeks and make a profound difference. Be one of those people. Leave a footprint.

···• Do just one thing

If you could do just one thing today that would make you a better leader, what would it be? It could be getting up at 5.30am to meditate, exercise and journal, so you go in to your day centred and clear about your purpose. It could be that each Wednesday you take someone in your team out for coffee, to discuss what is going on for them and how they are feeling about their work. Or it could be acting as a peer buddy and coach for a new member of your management team.

Pick one thing that you can start today, that will make you more effective as a leader, and then implement it for one month. See the difference that taking small steps on your leadership journey can make, to you, to people around you, and to your organisation. You might just start a revolution.

Leadership. Big word, but it's really not that scary, is it? We are all leaders, and we need to get mindful and purposeful about the type of leader we want to be, and can be, and then act on it. All of the content in this book will give you the tools you need to self-lead and to lead others. But only you can decide how you want to show up as a leader in your organisation, in your family, and in your life. Leadership is a gift, so please use it mindfully.

Getting real – *remember*

···• You don't need permission to lead. You don't need to be in a management role. You just need to decide, and then act.

···• Think about the type of leader you want to be. Spend some time thinking about the great leaders you admire, note down their qualities and behaviours, and determine how you can implement these in your life.

···• Be a role model. Do great things. Make a difference. Leave a footprint.

CHAPTER 20

Getting the basics right

Great things are not done by impulse,
but by a series of small things brought together.

– Vincent Van Gogh

O kay, I am going to warn you in advance – some of this is pretty basic. That's why I called the chapter *Getting the basics right* – pretty clever aren't I? Didn't need a Masters degree or two for that one. So, while you may roll your eyes and think I am crazy for including these topics in a book for upwardly mobile career women, pause for a minute while I tell you that I am flabbergasted (yes it's the only word that fits) by how many people, even senior people, in organisations and businesses of all types, just get this stuff wrong. And it can be very damaging to not only your reputation, but to your career. So bear with me, humour me if you have to, and let's consider what the basics look like, and what you need to be conscious of. I know you know all of this, but it might stimulate something that is helpful to be reminded of.

···• Be on time

This could be the most basic one of them all, and the one that I see so often is just not adhered to. Can someone please explain to me why this is so hard? Showing up when you commit to shows respect for others and respect for the importance of the meeting (even if you don't think it is, you still have to be there). There was a person I once worked with, who was always late for meetings. Always. He used to saunter in late, whether five minutes or 20 minutes, with no apology or even acknowledgement, often disrupting the flow of the meeting, and showing complete disrespect for those who managed to get there on time. I'm really sorry, but if the CEO can turn up on time, then get your ass into the room before the meeting starts. Seriously!

If you know you are going to be late, then make a call, send a text, or do what you need to do to alert the meeting organiser and send ahead your apologies. Slip into the meeting unobtrusively, don't ask that they do a complete recap for you, which completely disrupts the meeting, and catch up as you go. And next time, try to make allowances to be early. It shows that you are professional, courteous and that you respect your colleagues. It doesn't get much more basic than that.

···• Speaking of time, manage it

Managing your time is so important. We all have the same number of hours in the day, but some people manage to move mountains, while others just create a little molehill. There are heaps of tools and techniques to make better use of your time. Make a list of the three key things you have to do each day and do them first up in the morning, get up early, limit distractions like social networking, turn off your email alerts, do email only three times a day, and set specific times to return phone calls. You have heard them all before. The key thing is to analyse how effective you are being: are you getting the right things done, and are you making progress towards your goals? If you are, that's fantastic. If not, then take a look at how to maximise the time you have available, and how to get the most out it. Be smart with your time; you don't get it back again.

···• Learn to listen

Ah, the miracle that is the person who can actually listen, and not interrupt, talk over, or wait impatiently for you to stop speaking, so they can tell you what they think without even slightly taking into consideration anything you just said. Oh yes, I know you know this well. It is a rare person who has mastered the art of listening.

There is a saying that goes something like, *God gave you two ears and one mouth, use them accordingly.* That pretty much sums it up. Give people the respect of actually listening to what they are saying to you, not just pretending to. You will notice a massive shift in your relationships, and in the amount of information that people will share with you and how they will confide in you, if you just show up and shut up. People really just want to be heard. So hear them.

···• Do what you say you will

This is a good one. How many people do you know, whether they are in your team, your peer group, or even your boss at times, who say they will do something and then don't. I know plenty. And I am always so impressed when someone follows up, sends me the link to the report they said they would, calls to set up the coffee meeting they mentioned in passing, and delivers work when they say they will. Revolutionary, I know. If you want to stand out at work, then do what you say you will, when you say you will, and watch your star rise.

···• Give credit to others

Now this is one of my favourites. All those people out there who take credit for other people's ideas, thoughts, projects and work output – shame, shame, shame on you (no, no, not you of course, I know you wouldn't, but there are plenty out there who will, so beware). It is some of the worst behaviour I see in business, and is completely unacceptable. And there is no excuse. Some people do it without realising the impact and really don't mean harm by it.

But some people are just oh-so-calculating, know exactly what they are doing, and take any and every opportunity to pass off someone else's ideas or work as their own. So be mindful, please, never to be one of them, even unintentionally.

It could be as simple as acknowledging where the seed of an idea came from ... *we are pleased our proposal for a new strategy in this area has been accepted, and I wanted to thank Sarah for the original idea to proceed down this path.* Simple. Or it could be acknowledging the work of your team, or a peer group's team, when delivering your work.

I recently had a situation where I saw fantastic work being contributed behind the scenes by one work group, that was integral to the success of a major project. But when another department presented the work, the contributing team's work was hardly recognised, and the leader took all the credit. Not only did the contributing team feel completely demoralised, but they will also think twice before going out of their way for that leader again. It's just bad behaviour, and it is not forgotten. It doesn't need to be a grandiose gesture. Just make sure you give credit where credit is due. Oh, and one last point on this one – karma's only a bitch if you are. Just saying.

···· Say 'thank you'

In line with giving credit, is saying 'thank you'. So simple and easy, but so often forgotten. You work on a big project and as the next four projects line up behind it, you hardly have to time to breathe, as you are spinning on to the next one. Thanks? Who has time? You do.

We talked about gratitude in Chapter 9, so you already know the physiological and psychological benefits of expressing your thanks. But this is really just about good manners, recognising others efforts, and being kind. So say 'thank you' easily and often, and watch people light up as you acknowledge them. Your time will be well rewarded and you will feel just as good as your receiver.

···• Be a giver

We all have friends who are givers, and friends who are takers. And it's no different in the workplace. There are those who are always there to share information, lend a hand on a difficult project, and give input at a critical stage of a sales deal – all without expecting anything in return. And then there are those who just take, all of the time, never even thinking about giving back in return. They are the energy suckers of your workplace. They might be as nice as pie, and you may not even realise that they are sucking the lifeblood from you, but they are. So make sure you are a giver, and try and limit your exposure to the takers out there. Your energy will thank you for it.

···• Be prepared and consistent

How prepared are you for the meetings you go to every day? You may prepare really well for that big management presentation, but how much work do you do for other meetings that are seemingly less important?

I once had a mentee turn up to a mentoring meeting with me, without a pen and notebook. I mean seriously? If you are going to ask for someone's time, anyone's time, then show them the respect of thinking they might have at least one morsel of advice for you, that would be worth writing down. Made me not want to even open my mouth.

Or what about the team member, knowing that the CEO had asked for some important information, which you had had an additional meeting to clarify, who then turned up to the final preparation meeting looking like she didn't know what you were talking about and were sitting on the planet Mars. Really? Seriously, enough to drive me crazy! If you are employed to do a role, or you are servicing a client's requirements, then do the work. Be prepared. You won't get very far if you aren't.

···• Underpromise, overdeliver

Have you worked with those people who promise the world, and deliver, well, not much at all? They can talk a good game, but there really isn't much content under the surface, and they continuously let people down. Not a good look. There isn't much science to this; it is one of the simplest rules of career management. When committing to delivering work projects, it is always better to overestimate the time it will take, and under commit to the amount of work that will be delivered.

Now this may sound wrong, or even a little sneaky, but it's not. Think about it. Your boss asks you for a report to analyse last month's sales, and asks how long you will need to deliver it, and how many layers of data you can get to. You have a fair idea that you will be able to get to about five layers of numbers over the period, and that it will take you about three weeks. Now, if you tell your boss that, and you come even a little short on the content or miss the deadline by even a day, then she will be disappointed, and you will not have met her expectations. Not good for your career or your relationship. However, if you tell her that you will need four weeks and will get to three levels of data and she is happy about this, and you work hard to actually deliver it in three weeks at level five, you are a superstar. What would you prefer? You should always work to totally overachieve – even at your own highest level. Of course. But you need to manage expectations to succeed, and this is one of the key ways to do it.

So there you have it. Basic they are, but essential they will always be. So be mindful of these things, and you will be well on your way to being the rock star of your workplace.

Getting real – *remember*

···• We may think everyone behaves according to these standards, but take a look around your teams, peers and superiors, and you will know exactly what I am talking about.

···• Make getting the basics right, consistently, one of the differentiators to you and your brand, and the level of excellence you set for your personal behaviour at work.

···• You will not only set yourself up for success, but you will be a positive role model for others as well.

CHAPTER 21

Do what matters

Start by doing what's necessary; then do what's possible;
and suddenly you are doing the impossible.

– St. Francis of Assisi

Think about this scenario – you have been working for months on a special report for your boss, tirelessly slaving away, putting your heart and soul into the final output. You know that some of your other projects have slipped a little, but you really believe in the project you are working on, and you know (read: hope) your boss is going to be blown away by it. It's down to the crunch and it's time to present your report. When you do, your boss thinks it's good work, but is more concerned with project X that you have waiting in the slush pile, wants to know the status, and she needs it urgently – yep, like yesterday.

You walk out of her office feeling completely let down that there wasn't more of a positive song and dance about the report you had slaved over. And you are also now in a complete panic, due to the fact that she wants this other project delivered pronto, and you haven't even started it yet.

And with your head spinning and your self-confidence in the toilet, you are left wondering what on earth happened.

If this resonates with you at all, then you will hopefully know that you have fallen into the age-old trap of doing what you believe is the most important job of the moment, without checking in to see what the top priority is for the boss. We have all done this, myself included, and it is a pretty disheartening place to be. But there is a critical success lesson in this scenario: it is absolutely pointless doing great work, if it is not work that matters to the person who pays you. It's just a cold, hard fact.

We have many roles as career women. The most important, however, is to get the job that we are employed to do done, and done exceptionally well. No exceptions. Now whether you are self-employed and work for your clients, whether you have a boss in an organisation, or whether you run the company and report to the board and the shareholders, the fact remains the same. Losing sight of this is a potentially fatal mistake, and they don't come much bigger.

So, how can you ensure that you don't skip over this small detail, so you can excel in your role and keep building your rosy future? You need to have a really clear grasp on what your boss' expectations are. That's it. Now it sounds simple I know, but sometimes it can be easier said than done. We have the bosses who just want everything done and find it really hard to differentiate priorities, so you end up working all the hours in the universe and still find it hard to deliver to an acceptable standard. We have the bosses who say one thing, mean another, and then look at you like you are some crazy person, when you give them what they actually asked for. And of course, there are (I hate to say it) the purely incompetent bosses, who really don't know their ass from their elbow (sorry, it had to be said).

Most of us have had one or all of these bosses at some point in our careers. And although we may want to kill them, scream at them or throw large things at their heads, we still need to work out how to understand and meet their expectations, while keeping our sanity (and our pay packet) in check.

So what do we do?

I find the most effective way of managing a manager, is to clearly articulate in writing your understanding of the work priorities and the deliverables. Get crystal clear on what you believe them to be. Then have a meeting with your boss, preferably in person, but on the phone is fine, to review this list and agree for the coming period (one, three, six or 12 months) what you will focus on, and importantly, what you will deliver. If your manager goes off track, keep coming back to the written priorities you have laid out. You should also have an idea of your available time and energy for work commitments, so that if you get into a discussion about doing all of the things on the list (for boss #1 above), you can have a calm and clear conversation, knowing you have done the thinking and understand how much you can actually get done effectively. You also need to check in frequently, as we all know business priorities change, especially in the global economic and business climate we are in.

Now be prepared. Your boss might say that none of your priorities align with hers, and she wants you to zag left instead of right. That's fine, and better you know now, rather than in three months time, like our opening scenario, when your boss is really unhappy and you are really stressed.

At the end of the day, if you have signed up for a role – and let's hope that it's a role you love and is moving you on your way to your dream job (if you're not already there) – then you need to focus on what matters. So get clear, communicate it, and then get moving on delivering work that both you and your boss can be proud of.

Getting real – *remember*

···• Not having clearly defined and agreed expectations, between you and your boss, is a recipe for career disaster.

···• Write down your priorities and get your boss to agree with them, so you are both clear on the deliverables you have signed up for.

···• Be flexible – change happens. But if your boss is completely impossible, will not agree to defined expectations and you feel you cannot manage effectively because of it, think about getting a new boss. It is almost impossible to be effective in this environment. So think about your career short and long term, and find an exit strategy.

CHAPTER 22

Don't overcommit – plan mindfully

The main thing is to keep the main thing the main thing.

– Stephen Covey

Have you ever said 'yes' to many different things that, at the time, seemed perfectly reasonable and doable; but when it came to the crunch, you realised there was just no way you could manage it all? What am I saying? Of course you have – otherwise you probably wouldn't be reading this book.

As I write this, I find myself in exactly this situation, and it is not serving me well. The current list of things I willingly signed myself up for include (deep breath!):

···• day job, corporate role four days a week

···• committee member for major women's conference

···• speaker for women's conference, running four different sessions over two days (preparation, I hear you say? You bet. Sigh.)

···• co-lecturer in two post-graduate university programs – *Positive Psychology* and *Workplace Wellness*

···• co-producer of *The Wellness Project* TV – developing pitch, funding strategy and pilot for new wellness series

···• writing a book – yep, this one!

···• writing a book proposal to get this book published (I guess it was a good one, as here we are)

···• working on a concept for another book with my friend Michelle (actually, there is a series of three books – yes, yes I know)

···• building my new website

···• oh, add to that single mother, housekeeper, cook, yogi, meditator, coach, daughter, sister, friend, colleague and all around crazy person (this week at least)

So, you can see why I think this topic is an important one. Even those who really do know better (that would be me), still do this to ourselves from time to time, and it has consequences. Big ones. The consequences for me at the moment, other than the overwhelm and potential stress of it all, is that my body is telling me to just hang on a minute. It's not very happy, and is about to make a protest vote for a sit out. And who could blame it.

Why do we do this to ourselves? For me, in this situation, all of the projects are so exciting, and so exactly what I want to be focusing on right now. So I said 'yes' without really mapping out the consequences, or the timing, and the implications of that timing on my life. Let's face it; I didn't even pause to map them out, I just said 'yes'. As Michelle said to me this morning, *it's like sitting down to eat an amazing meal, and then eating so much you are stuffed and feel sick, because your eyes were bigger than your belly.* I want to be involved in all the amazing projects, however the planning needs to be mindful, so I don't end up with indigestion.

So for me, in this current situation, I have had to take stock. Luckily, this situation has only been going on for a few weeks (this time). So I am in the process of doing the following, which may help you if you get into this situation, or hopefully prevent you from getting into it, with better, more mindful planning.

So what am I doing about it? Looks like this:

1. Take a deep breath

2. Take another deep breath

3. Sit quietly and think about the following:
   a. What is on the 'to do' list?
   b. How much time will each project take? (Be real here or the whole exercise is pointless.)
   c. What sequence do things need to happen in?
   d. What can wait?
   e. What can come off the list?

4. Tune into what my body and spirit need at the moment, to sustain me and support me through this busy time

5. Keep breathing

And here is what I actually did:

1. Looked at my list and realised that these were all things that I want to do or be involved in, but I needed to get realistic about the time commitments and scheduling.

2. Went through each project and mapped out how many hours (in the real world, not my fantasy land) I needed to commit to each one.

3. Looked at what needed to happen when. The women's conference was the following week, so other than getting any critical business work out of the way, I focused for the next four days (preparation) and the following week (the event) solely on the event. This ensured I was focused on what needed to be done immediately, and meant that I was prepared, which lessened my stress considerably. I also committed that I would put no pressure on myself to write, organise

the website, or do anything else on the list that was not time critical for next week. Phew! Just those changes made things feel better and more manageable immediately.

4. As part of the above, I knew that the university work could wait for one more week. Once the conference came off my plate, I would have time to commit approximately four hours a week to my lecturing. I built this into my schedule on a weekly basis, so that it was programmed in, and I would not need to think/worry/stress about when it would get done. My WWP team and I also decided that we would put *The Wellness Project* TV work on hold for three weeks, until things settled down a little for each of us. A good decision, creating more headspace for me, and allowing me to focus on my speaking commitments. (Side note – a few weeks later, I actually took the lecturing off the plate for the moment, as I wanted to devote my time to other things, like writing this book). See, I said 'no' to something – big tick!

5. As the conference was coming off the list in a week's time, I didn't feel like anything else needed to be removed; but timing and scheduling would continue to be critical.

6. Regarding my body, I knew that I was in a state of needing nourishment and nurturing. I saw my integrative doctor, Dr. Marilyn Golden (who is brilliant and amazing, by the way) for some Biomesotherapy, some acupuncture and a Chinese herbal tonic. These things supported my system over the busy time. I also knew that my digestive system needed a rest, so it could work on building energy, not processing food.

So I did a few days on green juices, smoothies and all-round green stuff. This really nourished my body (and spirit) and helped give me the boost I needed. I don't do this very often. However, when I really need it, and actually do it, it has an amazing impact on me.

7. Also, I made sure that I meditated morning and night, went walking when I could, and did some gentle restorative yoga. Nothing strenuous, as this would only stress out my adrenals more. But gentle exercise energises me, while also allowing rest.

So there you have it. I kept hearing a voice in my head this week saying, *we teach what we most need to learn.* This could not be truer. These things – taking stock, prioritising, decommitting, nurturing ourselves – they are not easy. If they were, we would all be getting it right all of the time. But they matter. We cannot be successful and well, if we are not mindful about what we take on, why we do what we do, and where we want to spend our precious energy.

Learning to be mindful, and planning our days and our lives consciously, is a critical skill that can be learnt, built and honed. It is a key to leading successful, happy, healthy and whole lives. And when we get off track like I did here, we gently and lovingly remind ourselves where we want to be. And where we want to be is having this gift of an amazing career, being well in the process and living the life we love. And so we adjust our course. And it feels better already.

Getting real – *try this*

···· Take stock – what is on your plate at the moment? Take a real look at what you have going on, so you have a clear view, not a 'compromised by stress' view of your world.

···• Prioritise and decommit – first, what can come off your list? It is very rare, when I ask this question to people, that there isn't at least one thing that can come off. And it's usually many things that they realise are just not important – like my uni lecturing. When you have your clean list, prioritise it, like I did in my example. Set realistic time expectations, communicate with those who matter, and then focus on the tasks at hand. You will feel better, think clearer and get more done.

···• Support yourself – what do you need at this time to support your body, mind and spirit? Think about the nurturing practices you can build into your day, the food you can eat, the restorative practices you can do, to help you through your commitments. By nurturing yourself, you will ensure you are able to keep on keeping on, and achieve all you want to in a healthy way.

CHAPTER 23

Making moves, making choices

Life is the sum of all your choices.

– Albert Camus

When you think about your career, do you ever feel like you are in a massive rush to get to your next career destination, and you just can't get there fast enough? Or perhaps you feel like you are stuck in a career mud pile up to your waist and can't move forward, even if your life depended on it. Many of us have felt like one or both of the above at some time in our careers. I certainly have.

In the early stages of my career, around the time I was in the mix of my first big management role, I was so hungry for the next job, the next promotion, and the next experience, that I almost jeopardised the role I was in. If I had jumped too soon into the next role, I wouldn't have had the set of experiences I had, learnt the skills I developed, or met the people that would eventually take me into my next company. What I couldn't see at the time, but see so clearly now, is that I was building the foundations that would set a solid base for the rest of my career. Lucky my intuition kicked in, and I stayed put until it really was time to move.

Of course, impatience has a twin sister. Sometimes, we sit too long, stay so long in a role that we become stale, tired, and lethargic, and so does our work. And that doesn't do any favours for anyone, least of all ourselves. We need to stay fresh, vibrant and energised; and we need to time our workloads and our roles to manage that energy.

Timing really is everything.

So how do we find that balance, and get that mix right, so that we can work the timing in our favor?

Firstly it helps to understand the reasons why we rush ahead, and also get a handle on the reasons we might stay stuck for too long. So, here is my summation on why you may feel the need to race to the next big thing, and some reasons why we might let the daisies grow under our desk (and turn to weeds).

Now it's really important for me to say that there is no judgement in any of this. None. Many of us have been here at varying levels and at different times in our careers. However, for us to move forward and follow our passion, we need to take action. It starts, as always, with being really honest about where you are right now. From there, you can chart a course forward. Let's see if you can relate to any of this.

···• Five key reasons we rush ahead

1. Feeling uncomfortable – Something is going on in our current role that we don't want to deal with, so we figure it's easier to leave.

2. Fear of missing out – We worry we will miss out on the next great thing.

3. Driving ambition – We desperately want to get ahead, get to the next experience, and nab that next promotion.

4. Impatience – We think we are ready now, and we just don't want to wait.

5. Over-confidence – We think we have learnt all there is to learn, where we currently are.

If you can relate to any of the above, I suggest you ask yourself the following questions – and be really honest with the answers you give yourself. These are the types of questions I ask people who I coach or mentor, when they are itching to get to their next role, so we can get clear on their intention. They are applicable to anyone, at any stage of their career. Think about these:

···• How long have you been in your role?

···• What did you want to achieve in this role, when you went in to it? What was your goal?

···• Have your achieved that goal? Can you articulate it and quantify the result? Does your manager/mentor/sponsor agree?

···• Have you developed all of the skills you needed to build in this role?

···• Have you built all of the needed relationships and connections, from where you currently are in the business?

···• Is there another reason you are feeling itchy, like a performance issue, relationship challenge, or a deliverable you don't think you can meet?

···• Are you crystal clear on where you want to move to next, how you will get there, and where it will fit in your career plan?

These are all important questions, and they lead to important answers. Kidding yourself, or lying to yourself is not helpful to you, your employer or your career. So when you get that urge to rush on ahead, change your role, or even change your whole career, sit down and give it some real thought. Get in touch with your intuition, your gut, as well as your rational mind (brilliant as it is!) and work out what your driver is. When you can answer these questions, you will be clear on the direction you need to move in, and for the right reasons.

Now, if you are not in a massive hurry to rush ahead, you may be at the opposite end of the spectrum – you may be stuck in the mud. To see if this may be true for you (or for a team member, or a friend), let's look at some of the reasons for staying put for too long.

···• **Five reasons we stay stuck**

1. Feeling comfortable – We are settled where we are and it's too much hassle to move on.

2. Fear of the unknown – The devil you know is better than the scary unknown world.

3. Lack of direction – We don't know where we are going career-wise, so we do nothing.

4. Complacency – We think the future will take care of itself.

5. Apathy – We are just doing our job to pay the rent/ mortgage/school fees, and we just can't be bothered looking for something better.

And the questions to ask? Have a think about some of these – you can also use these with your team, people you mentor, or a friend you may be helping with a career issue:

···• What is it you are feeling about your current role? Is it a positive emotion like excitement, or a negative emotion like boredom?

···• If it is excitement, you are probably in the right place for now, and not stuck at all, so you are off the hook.

···• If it is boredom or apathy, think back to a time when you did feel excited about your work – what was happening for you then, that is not happening now? See if you can pinpoint it, and recreate it.

···• Are you feeling like you just don't know what to do next? If so, go back and revisit your strengths, and see if they can point you in another direction. And on strengths, if you are feeling bored, look at ways you can use your strengths in new and interesting ways in your work – it might be enough to re-engage you, or to propel you toward your next role.

···• If you are feeling complacent about your career, you may have lost touch with your passion and purpose. Spend some time revisiting both of these, in the context of what you want to be doing with your work. It may stimulate your next move. As I said earlier (actually Oprah said it), once you discover what your purpose is, the way to do it often becomes clear.

So there is some food for thought about timing. One other important thing to mention on this topic is about taking risks. I see so many women who stay in a role they have long grown out of, because they are too scared to take the next step. Again, there is no judgement here; we all have fear of failure and fear of the unknown. Women are also sometimes less prone than men to put themselves forward for that promotion, or enter into a completely new area of the business, like a line role from marketing, preferring to stay on the back line. Think about the reasons why you may be risk adverse, and work out whether the fear is a real one, or just a voice in your head telling you not to try.

Hopefully, you are in exactly the right place and moving at exactly the right pace at the moment, and things are going swimmingly. I hope that is the case. But if you find yourself in one of the above categories, then spend a little time (read: more than five minutes) and work through the reasons and the questions. You might be surprised what comes up, when you give yourself permission, time and space to invest in finding the answers. And then you can chart your course, knowing you have done the work to come up with the right answer.

Getting real – *remember*

···• It doesn't pay to make rash career decisions. If you are feeling the urge to jump, sit down first and really consider your motivation before doing anything you may regret later. Sometimes, the best opportunities are the ones you leave too soon. And you can't often go back.

···• If you realise you are stuck, do something about it. It can spell career disaster to not only sit in a role for too long, but to be seen to do so. The longer you sit, the harder it is to rebuild your momentum. So recognise this sign early, and get moving.

···• Master the art of listening – to yourself. You know the answer, when it comes to where you are in your career. You just need to get quiet enough to hear it.

PART THREE

Becoming Well Women

Love yourself first and everything else falls into line.
You really have to love yourself to get anything
done in this world.

– Lucille Ball

So where are you at with your health and wellbeing? No, don't just give me the flippant, off the cuff, everything is fine (FINE) answer. I want you to sit and think about it for a few minutes (please). How do you feel in your body? What is the state of your mind? How are your energy levels? What do you feel like when you go to bed at night, and how do you feel when you wake up in the morning? How well are you eating? How are your relationships and connections going? It's okay, spend a few minutes thinking about it now. Don't worry; I'll be here when you get back.

So, what did you come up with? Are you truly feeling well, nurturing and nourishing yourself with beautiful whole foods, getting regular exercise, eight hours of sleep a night, meditating daily, doing some yoga, having restorative time, spending quality time with your family and friends, and connecting with your community? You are? Oh, that's just fantastic! You can probably skip this part of the book then, or just use it as a refresher.

Now, for the 99.9% of us who aren't consistently living like this (!) this part of the book is so critical. Because no matter how strong your personal attributes, no matter how great your career, nothing is sustainable if you are not well. Truly well. Healthy. Restored.

Connected. Nurtured. I know this is the part most of us struggle with, and it is the part that I struggle with too. Even though I have so much of the cognitive knowledge around psychology, wellness, yoga, meditation, nutrition and so on, the actual part of putting it into practice remains a challenge for me. Yes, I am getting better. Yes, I do most of the above things most days. But it is by conscious, mindful choice, and it takes consistent effort. That's just the truth of it. And it's the truth for most of us.

The first, most important part of getting well, is getting real. Brutally, soul baring, real. We cannot move forward with integrity, if we do not get real with our authentic self, and understand what is going on for us right now. Not last year, not last week, but today. Right here, right now.

To illustrate this, I somewhat painfully share the following excerpt from my musings one night, many moons ago, when I had just had enough. Enough of the excuses, the lies I kept telling, the hiding and the delusion. So I decided to get real. I couldn't sleep, so I got up at 11.30pm to sit at my computer and see what came out. And this is what did. For me, it's about as real as it gets.

Sunday, 11.30pm
So it's been a hard few weeks. There, I said it. Actually if truth be told, it's been a pretty hard year. While I have had some major successes, my body has taken the toll of my success. I think I have been in denial about the state of my health, yet again. Because of this, I have been mindless, and have ended up in a complete and utter mess. Again. Oh boy. So let's get real shall we? I have autoimmune disease. I have arrhythmia and thyroid disease. I have had, and still have, adrenal fatigue. And while these things do not define me, I cannot just continue to drive and drive myself, and eat crap, and drink alcohol and eat countless amounts of sugar, and think that I should still feel well. Really? Who am I kidding? A healthy person who operated the way I do most of the time, would feel like shit. Never mind my health issues.

Why does it take us so long to wake up? For me, it's been at least a decade, depending on how you count it. Longer than that, if you count my chronic fatigue at 21. That was the first sign that the way I was living was not working. It was the first sign that I should create a different life for myself. A life that would enable calm and create wellbeing. Instead, I created a life led by my insatiable drive, and it has led to a life of ill health, and again, to be honest, unhappiness.

But I know that the first step, the critical step, the do-it-before-anything-will-shift step, is to be well. To be truly well. To put myself first, my health and wellbeing first, and to be honest enough with myself to know that I haven't been. And it is time. Far beyond time, one would think. But we act when we are ready, and I am ready now. Ready to be honest, ready to be real, ready to heal. Ready to be the best I can be, in the best health of my life, and be the best version of myself.

PS: Oh, and note to self – if you want to be fit and healthy and well (and lose all that weight), you need to move your ass. Just saying ...

Hmmm, nice huh? Among the pain of that writing is the fact that it is a place to move forward from, because it is reality. My reality. It is not the story I kept telling myself in my head; it is not my excuses and my old patterns; and it is not what I wanted to believe. It is the truth. It is (was) my life, and that is the only place we can start from.

We must start from where we are. So before you get into this section of the book, I invite you to spend some time thinking about where you are now. What is really going on for you at the moment, in all of the areas I listed at the start of this section – nutrition and nourishment, exercise, mindset, restoration, sleep, relationships and connection. What would 'getting real' look like for you? I invite you to be brave, be bold and be true. We start from where we are. So, make a start right here. And then when you are ready, when you are real, let's get started on creating true wellbeing.

CHAPTER 24

Inhale, exhale, repeat

Smile, breathe and go slowly.

– Thich Nhat Hanh

I remember a time, years and years ago, when I was trying yoga for the first time. I vividly recall the teacher telling us, in that slow, calm, yogic voice, that we were going to learn to breathe. Breathe. Really? I remember thinking, *Seriously? What do you think I have been doing my entire life?* and thinking it was all a load of rubbish. I knew how to breathe; I really didn't need to pay fifteen bucks to be taught. I obviously wouldn't blame you, if you were having the same reaction reading this.

But let me ask you to hold your judgement for just a few moments, while we explore this a little. When was the last time you took a mindful breath? I mean a really deep inhalation and a slow, long exhalation, while being fully present? I can tell you that, even now, I can sometimes go a whole day on autopilot, and get to the end of it and feel like I haven't really taken a conscious breath the entire day.

So before we go any further, let's try this. Sit and close your eyes for a moment. Well actually, read this and then close your eyes (silly me!). I want you to breathe in while counting to four, hold for a moment, and then breathe out to the count of four and hold for a moment. Go on, trust me, it won't hurt, and you may just enjoy it.

Repeat the breath sequence five times. Go on, I will be here when you get back …

There you go. You have just breathed mindfully. You have taken a real breath, while being present and conscious. While you just completed a magical, yogic four-part breath sequence, you have also engaged the relaxation response, which means you have turned off the fight or flight mechanism in your body, that is a reaction to stress.

While that may not be very meaningful to you at the moment, what should be meaningful is that just by doing that one sequence, you may feel calmer and more present, and it is as easy as breathing. Breathing mindfully.

It's amazing the impact this can have, not only on yourself, but also on those around you. One of my favourite things to do in meetings, when stress levels may be rising and some tempers may be getting to boiling point, is to actually stop the meeting, and gently remind people to breathe. Now you can imagine in my wellness world, people would find this quite normal and happily proceed. But picture for a moment a stuffy boardroom, filled with stiff people in suits, all being very proper and important. And I tell them to breathe. Funnily enough, just saying it can have a very calming effect and can completely change the energy in the room. Now it's not always possible (and in some meetings I just wouldn't dare), but when it works, it works a treat.

····• **The art and science of the breath**
We know that we breathe to stay alive, and that it is an automatic body function. Our cells need oxygen, and carbon dioxide needs to be expelled from the body. Yes, we know that's the boring stuff we learnt in science class! What is cool though, is that while breathing is automatic and most people don't give it a second thought, we can control it and change its rate. And learning to do this effectively, can in fact be life-changing.

Many ancient traditions, such as yoga and tai chi, have long known about the power of the breath, and that the breath is the link between mind and body. Some traditions also believe that spiritual awakening can be found through conscious breathing. For those sceptics among you, you can breathe easy, knowing that science also now tells us that breathing correctly can promote health and wellbeing. It helps us manage stress and related conditions, by soothing the autonomic nervous system.

Controlled, mindful breathing promotes relaxation, and triggers that thing called the relaxation response. This turns off the fight or flight reaction we have to stress – think running away from a tiger (or your boss), when in a situation of perceived danger. When we are breathing in a relaxed manner, our breathing is generally through the nose, and is calm, slow, even and gentle. In times of stress, when our breath tends to be in our chest and very short and sharp, we can consciously mimic a relaxed breathing pattern, to trigger this relaxation response in our bodies. I do this often, and it has a profound effect on me, even in those moments when I am flustered, like before a major presentation (especially then, actually). The autonomic nervous system controls the bodily functions, and our relaxed breathing can trigger many of them, including lowering our blood pressure, reducing nasty stress hormones such as cortisol and adrenalin, improving immune function, increasing our energy levels, and increasing our feelings of calm and general wellbeing.

If that isn't enough motivation to get you focusing on your breath, then consider this: promoting relaxation through mindful, controlled breathing can potentially lessen a huge number of disorders, including anxiety, asthma, chronic fatigue syndrome, chronic pain, panic attacks, skin conditions, high blood pressure and of course, stress.

This will hopefully entice you to try some new breathing techniques, not just for yourself, but for your loved ones too. I spend time with my son on his breathing, as part of our regular meditation practice, and especially at times when he is upset or stressed out (and, god forbid, those times when he's having a major crack attack – read, pre-teen mood swings). It is a wonderful way to teach our kids, and ourselves, to self-sooth in times of need, when there may not be any other mechanism for us to do so.

Giving ourselves the time and permission to fully, mindfully breathe, is one of the most gentle, kind, loving things we can do for ourselves, and in turn, for those around us. And it is one of the most profound ways we can positively impact on our wellbeing.

So, breathe like the goddesses you are, ladies. It may just change your lives.

···• Conscious breathing practice

Lie on your back, or sit comfortably in a chair, and close your eyes. Place one hand on your belly, and the other hand on your chest. Breathe in and out through your nose (if you can, or through your mouth is fine). Don't change anything, just notice your breath. How does it feel? Smooth or ragged, shallow or deep, chest heavy or belly breathing? Now, take another breath, and consciously move your breath into your belly. Abdominal breathing helps us with the relaxation response, so let's induce that now. Breathe into your belly for a count of four, hold for a moment, and then exhale for a count of four. Pause. Continue breathing in this way for a few minutes, or as long as you choose, noticing your hand on your belly rising and falling with your breath. Use this practice whenever and wherever you need, to get focused and centred. After a while, you will be able to do this throughout your day naturally, with wonderful effect.

Getting real – *try this*

···• Become mindful of your breath throughout your day. Think about where in your body your breath flows into; how does it feel when you inhale and exhale; where do you feel expansion when you breathe; is your breath slow, fast, ragged, smooth; does your breath reach your belly or remain in your chest? Thinking about these questions, will help you become more conscious of your breathing.

···• Witness how becoming more aware of your breathing throughout your day, changes how you feel. Do you feel calmer, more peaceful, less frazzled? Watch and notice any changes through your enhanced consciousness.

···• Actively practise your breathing, as outlined in the exercise in this chapter. Hold it lightly, watch it expand and relish your breath as a tool you can use, to ease yourself through your days.

CHAPTER 25

Learn to meditate

You cannot stop the wave, but you can learn to surf.

– Jon Kabat-Zinn

In this chapter, we are going to learn about meditation. I am going to teach you how to sit in lotus pose every day, for one hour in the morning and one hour in the evening. You will learn how to completely clear your mind of any and all thoughts and become Zen, like a monk. You will learn how to chant the perfect *Om*, which you will repeat one hundred times a day. You will get up at 4am every day to do this, but it will be so worth it, you won't mind at all.

Stop the clock. Oh, sorry, that's not my book! I forgot that my book is the practical, live in the real world, get to learn how to really integrate this stuff. So we might not go that hardcore just yet. Sorry if I scared you. Of course, if you want to do the above, feel completely free. It will change your life. But if you're not that way inclined just yet, then let's take a more gentle approach, shall we?

Meditation. It is such a simple word, yet it puts the fear of God into so many people, just by saying the word. Med-it-a-tion. *Have you tried meditating*, I said to the extremely stressed out, ready to jump off the building, executive, *Oh yeah, I tried that once, couldn't stop the thoughts in my mind, so it's not for me. I can't meditate.* Hmmm. If I, or any meditation teacher, had a dollar for every time we have heard that one, we would be filthy rich. Rolling in it. Or there is this one, to the stressed out friend: *Have you tried any of those meditations you asked me for? I downloaded them on your iPod for you.* Response. *Oh yes I will, Megan. Just not right now, as I am so stressed out and busy, I really can't cope with anything new, I have so much on my mind.* Exactly.

So why should we bother, I hear you ask? A few of the reasons I meditate, are for the stillness it creates for me, the sense of peace it generates, and the nourishment I feel in body, mind and soul, both during and after my practice. It doesn't even have to be a long practice to get these benefits, as even five minutes can do the trick.

From a scientific perspective, a massive amount of research has been conducted into the power and benefits of meditation on the brain, the body, and everything in between. You might want to take a deep breath now; it's a long list. Meditation has been proven to make your brain stronger, help manage stress, and improve your immune system. Also, it can help you lose weight by helping to control your eating habits, it can improve kids' test scores, it improves our ability to tune out distractions – and, wait for the climax – it can make you look better and improve sex (yep, I know that last one got your attention). What else could you possibly need to know?

Now before you race off to buy a meditation cushion and get your Om on, let me share a few more important things with you. Let's start by dispelling the first myth about meditation. The end game of your meditation practice, at least initially, is not to completely empty your mind of all its thoughts and busy-ness. In fact, I am not sure if that ever happens. Well, maybe if you are Thich Nhat Hanh or Matthieu Ricard, Buddhist monks with decades of experience. But for us everyday lay people, meditation is mostly about showing up, getting still, and following the breath. And there is no such thing as meditating the right way, or the wrong way. There is only doing it, or not doing it.

To paint this picture for you, let me relay what happened in my morning meditation today, which I have come straight from. It was ten minutes long, and went something like this:

> Sit on meditation cushion. Wriggle around (a lot). Fiddle with Zen timer on my iPad. Start timer. Get ready to clear my mind. I am *so* ready to do this. My mind has other plans ... you have to do all that shopping today ... don't forget to get some sleeping tea as you will need it while you are travelling ... Luca really does need a new jacket for the snow, his old one is too small, so just go get him one today ... I wonder if I can get a pair of skinny jeans that I like, as I really need them to be able to tuck inside my knee-length boots, leggings will just be too cold ... breathe ... in through the nose, feel the cool air coming in, down into the belly, oh that feels good, out through the nose ... god, those birds are so loud out there this morning, I wonder what is going on ... Luca is still sleeping, he was really tired last night ... chime, chime, chime ... time is up.

You get the picture. What a shocker. Some days you turn up for your meditation practice and it is exactly like this. It just is. But the point is that you have shown up. You have sat down. You have breathed. And you have been still (even if your mind wasn't). This is why it is called practice.

And some days it is very different. Yesterday, I sat down, turned the timer on (or so I thought) and went straight into a deep meditation, while focusing on my breath. I had thoughts come in, but instead of getting on the thought train with them, I let them pass me by, and stayed with my breath. It was all very Zen. The random thought that did pop in a few times was, *I wonder when that meditation timer will go off, it is meant to chime at the five minute interval. Oh well, I really have only been sitting here for a minute, back to my breath.* In fact, when I came out of the meditation, the timer had not been set, and I had been sitting there for 20 minutes in bliss. It felt like two minutes.

This is just the path. We cannot expect to sit down, be completely tranquil, clear of the thousands of thoughts we continually think on any given day, and go into a Zen-like trance, all in ten minutes, when we first start to show up. Let's get real here. This doesn't happen for most of us instantly, and it doesn't happen every time we sit down. But it does happen. When it does, you feel so clear, and free and peaceful. And here is the strange thing. Even when I have a practice like I had today, I still feel that way. I feel grounded. When I begin to meditate, I can literally feel myself drop into my body. I don't know where from, but I can feel myself coming back, my legs get heavy, my shoulder blades drop down my back, the weight is lifted off, and I am here. Here now.

So I am hoping by now you want a piece of this too, right? Maybe just take it out for a spin and see what happens? I am seeing you nodding vigorously, and you can't wait to get started. To help you out, I share here two meditation practices and two book recommendations for you, so you can start to play with this a little.

···• Breath Meditation

This is probably the most accessible meditation, and it is one I do everyday, both in my formal morning and evening practice, and throughout the day, to bring me into a state of mindfulness. Sit comfortably, close your eyes, and bring your attention to your breath. Breathe in and out through your nose (if you can) and follow the breath with your attention. That's it. Deceptively simple, isn't it? When your mind wanders, and it will, gently bring your attention back to your breath. Sit for as long as you like – even five minutes can be transformative.

···• Guided Meditation

When starting a meditation practice, it is often challenging to still the mind, even momentarily (as my story above highlights). It can be really helpful to have something to focus your attention on. I regularly use a guided visualisation, which is a recording of someone leading you through a meditation practice. It can be a beautiful experience. Some of my favourites come from the Chopra Centre, and they are mostly free to download. Thanks to Deepak, for sharing these gifts with the world. Check out my website for links.

Opening to Meditation: a gentle, guided approach (book and cd), by Diana Lang was one of the first books I ever bought on meditation, when I was at a health retreat, trying to de-stress my (then) crazy life. The guided meditations that come with this book are still some of my most treasured ones.

The Miracle of Mindfulness: an introduction to the practice of meditation, by Thich Nhat Hanh, a world-renowned Zen master. In this, his most popular book, Thich Nhat Hanh helps us find calm, by taking hold of our consciousness. While that may sound daunting, he leads us down this path through practical instruction and daily, moment-to-moment awareness. I love this book – the simple, age-old wisdom, shared from a kind and loving heart.

Getting real – *remember*

···• Begin. You can start with just five minutes twice a day, and gradually build it up to ten or twenty. No need to rush or push yourself, you have a lifetime. And remember, it's five minutes, and you do have time. Just do it (please).

···• Make a commitment. It's called meditation practice for a reason, you need to show up, every day.

···• Keep breathing. Focus on your breath in meditation. This will transfer over into your daily life, and it will change more than your busy mind.

CHAPTER 26

Listen to your inner voice

At the centre of your being you have the answer; you know who you are and you know what you want.

– Lao Tzu

When you need to make a decision, how do you make up your mind? Do you talk to lots of people? Talk to just a few trusted confidantes? Call your mum maybe? Listen to no-one and just rush on in, on a wing and a prayer? Or do you, by chance, trust your instincts? Do you possibly take a moment to get really quiet, away from all the noise of your busy world, and just listen to *yourself?* To that voice inside you, somewhere deep down inside your gut, that tells you what you already know to be true, if you were only to get quiet enough to hear it.

If you do, I applaud you. But if you aren't there yet, don't worry; you are not alone. So many people wouldn't know the difference between their own voice and a stampede of elephants, especially when the voices of others can be so loud, it is impossible to hear anything other than their screaming diatribe (well, at least it sounds like a scream inside my head, but that could just be me). This is especially true for those who are invested in an outcome, based on your choices – a parent, spouse, boss, friend, even your child. You name it, anyone who has a stake in what happens to you, will have a voice and an opinion about what you should do or who you should be at any given hour of the day. I know, trust me – I have enough voices in my head sometimes, that I think I am a constant re-run of the movie *Sybil*, but on steroids – Sally Field has nothing on my voices!

But here is the thing, and there really is no way of getting around it. The only person who knows what is best for you, truly, truly best for you, is you. And the only way you can get in touch with that knowledge, is to get really quiet, and to listen.

So why is it so hard for us to follow our instincts and tune in to our own wisdom? Well, for starters, many of us have ignored our inner voice for so long; we are so out of touch it is unrecognisable. You know what it's like when you so constantly take advice from others, that you don't even bother to tune in to yourself. What's the point, right, everyone else has the answers?

And then there is the trust issue. Even women who are in touch with their inner voice – meaning they can recognise it when it starts up a conversation – have lost the self-confidence required to make a decision based on their inner guidance. So they second guess themselves to death, or eventually just give up and move on to the nearest piece of reasonably sound advice they can find. It's much easier that way, right?

Wrong and wrong.

While it is all fine and good to take input from those who are close to you, it is not okay to just take their advice and act on it, without looking inside first to see what *you* think is right for you. I have been in this trap before, and I was there for many long years. I have people who are very close to me, who know me very well. They also have very strong opinions about how I should live my life, and what is best for me. Of course they do. They love me and want me to be happy. But for many years, I gave far too much air time to their voices, and little or no time to mine, and I got steered all over the ship, on a course that could have been much more direct had I only trusted myself.

You can give all of that responsibility away, letting others tell you what you should think, what you should do, who you should marry, which career you should be in, and what job you should take next. You can do that. Sometimes it is a pretty easy out, saving you from having to really think about what you want, and from having to take responsibility for the outcome. Someone else told you to do it, so blame them. You know how that game goes, and we can all play it very well.

But why not be brave instead. Why not get real, get quiet, tune in, and listen to yourself. You can fast track yourself through a world of wrong decisions: bad boyfriends, even a divorce or two, not to mention the wrong job, and dare I say it, a disastrous outfit, if you just trust yourself. Now of course, that doesn't mean that your choices will never steer you wrong – and bad shoes, as well as bad bosses, do happen to good women – but at least the decisions will be yours and yours alone.

So, how do we get to this place of listening to our intuition, trusting our gut, and acting on it? The best way I know is through meditation. You knew I was going to say that, right? It's not that scientific – well actually, there is science behind it, but you don't even need to go there. The only place you need to go is to your mat. Or to your meditation cushion, your chair under the tree in the backyard, beside the ocean, or on the open road with your running shoes on. Anywhere you can find that peace and silence, and where you can get really quiet with yourself and listen. That is where you will tune in to your intuition. And it pays to listen. So get quiet, tune in to yourself, your truth, your knowing, and you will tap into a power that is far beyond the best advice you could pay for in the whole universe – because it is yours.

Getting real – *try this*

···• I was in yoga class this morning, lying on my mat, and my beautiful teacher, Lucy Proud, guided us to turn our ears inward, as if they were sitting in the middle of our heads. This was a great image for me, to guide my listening to what was going on inside, not on the outside. Practise this in your meditation, and see how you feel and what you tune in to. Even better, place your ears in your heart or in your stomach, where your inner wisdom comes from. Beautiful.

···• Meditate. We have already covered this in Chapter 25, so I know you are all now racing to your cushions to get your Om on. But seriously, it is the best way to get in touch with your inner voice, so get quiet every day, and listen.

···• Learn to trust yourself. You, and only you, know what is best.

CHAPTER 27

There is no stress, only stressful thoughts

We don't see things as they are, we see them as we are.

– Anaïs Nin

I read this line a few years ago – there is no stress, only stressful thoughts – and I thought it was a joke. I kept reading for the punch line. Only there wasn't one. Then I got a little cranky. Truth be told, I wanted to slap someone (gently, of course). Who could be stupid enough to say something like that? There is no stress. How ridiculous. Whoever wrote that, I thought to myself, clearly doesn't live in the real world, where there are jobs, kids, school fees, bosses to deliver for, dreams that are yet to be fulfilled and a never-ending to do list that 'must be done NOW', that never seems to get done. Sound familiar? No stress? Who was he kidding? (I assumed of course that a man must have written these words, as any woman would, of course, know that this statement was CRAZY!).

But once I had picked myself up from the floor and was over the absurdity of the comment, my inquisitive, analytical side kicked in, and I had to know if this could be true. Could it? Could stress really be completely of our own doing, and within our control to stop? What would this mean? That so many years of my life spent spinning on a stress-induced merry-go-round was a state that could have been avoided, if only I could have controlled my thoughts? That I could have just gotten off the ride? Really?

Now I am a fairly intellectual person. So, once I thought about this for a while, pondered it really, I got it. Meaning I got it on an intellectual level. But that is a little different from getting it on a physical, in the real world, stuck in the thick of it, level. You know what I mean. Like when you are late for work, your kids aren't even dressed yet let alone fed, you haven't made the school lunches, Johnny is having a meltdown in the corner because he can't find his favourite pencil, and you have a meeting with your boss starting in, oh, one hour, that you haven't yet prepared for. Let's see. Stress is all in my head. Not. Very. Helpful.

Or is it? If we could alter our perspective and view stress, not as something that is done to us, that happens to us, but something that we can in fact manage with some planning, forethought and strategies, wouldn't that be incredibly empowering? To know that we really don't need to be victims of our circumstances, that we can take charge and manage our days and our lives, without the constant battle with the stress gremlins running havoc in our heads, not to mention creating chaos with our nervous systems? So let's hang with that thought for a minute. Just breathe into the possibility of that, for just a moment. How would that feel? Pretty amazing, right? Liberating. Potentially even life-changing.

In fact, controlling my stress, or controlling the thoughts in my head that lead me to believe I am stressed (note the difference), has been life-changing for me. I have spent a lot of time over the past decade, learning about self-development and personal thriving. I consider myself a fairly educated person. I have a couple of masters degrees, one in wellness no less; I am qualified to teach yoga and meditation; I read voraciously; and I coach people on their wellbeing and how to create their best life. But it wasn't always that way. In fact, it used to be pretty much the opposite. And it wasn't a fun place to be.

For years, I used to rush out of the house every morning, looking like a crazy person, because by the time I had gotten up, showered, dressed, got my son organised for school, made breakfast (on a good day), packed the bags for the day, got my work stuff together, got Luca into the car and plopped myself in the driver's seat, I was completely exhausted. I felt like I had run a marathon, and it was usually only 7.30am. And more often than not, the scene ended in tears, either my son's or mine (or both). Not the best version of myself. I hated and dreaded this part of my day, and had uttered under my breath more than once *I am not (add expletive) doing this for the rest of my life.* I was so stressed; I actually ended up with adrenal exhaustion and complete burnout. You have already heard my story. I had to take sick leave, change my job, and literally change my life, as it was just not working. And it should never have come to that.

What I realise looking back on that time, with the knowledge and practices that I now have to manage myself more effectively, is that while my life was incredibly busy, it was actually the way I looked at it, the dialogue that was a continual loop in my head, and the impact this was reaping on my existence, that were the key issues. And while I was in the driver's seat all along, I just didn't know where the keys were.

So what do we do? Well, we have to get those gremlins in our heads under control, that is for sure. Here are some of my top techniques for getting your stressful thoughts under control, and managing yourself with kindness, love and patience.

···• Activate your power thoughts

This is a biggie. Do you pay attention to that voice in your head, the one that is usually telling you all the things you are doing wrong, where you were meant to be 15 minutes ago, that your thighs are fat, and generally how hopeless you are at everything? Yes you know the one. Well, I hate to break it to you, but that voice is you. And you can learn to turn it off, turn down the volume, lessen the frequency, or even change the channel.

One of the most important tools you have in your kit, to keep calm and carry on, is to manage your internal dialogue. Louise Hay says so beautifully, *every thought I think is creating my future.* Louise has dedicated her life to helping the world understand that, by lovingly managing the thoughts we think, we can create the life we want to live. Our power thoughts are the positive thoughts we affirm, to create that future.

Around about the time I was coming out of my stress-induced nightmare, I knew I had to ramp up my ability to think differently. I began to choose a positive affirmation every time I started on my downward spiral of stress-induced, maddening thoughts. That affirmation was *peace and happiness.* Oh my God, if I had a dollar for every time I have uttered those words, in my head or out loud. I laugh now, but it helped smooth the path to the new life I was creating, and the new thought patterns I used to support the process. I became calmer, more peaceful, and yes, happier, because I had changed the dialogue in my head.

The other one I have been using for about a year and a half now is *I am on my purposeful path and I live with grace and ease.* Beautiful. It has really helped me to actually find my purposeful path, and change a lifelong belief that things have to be hard won, to be achieved and valued. It was an old tape that needed changing, and this affirmation helped me to do that. And what do you know, things have become so much easier, because that is now the outlook I have, and the barometer with which I view my choices.

When we create a positive affirmation and use it, especially at times when we can feel the gremlins about to kick in, we short circuit that negative cycle, and give the mind something else to focus on – the positive thought – and we go on an upward spiral instead. And it doesn't all have to be so serious. I have a girlfriend, who sometimes gets nervous before walking in to a big boardroom meeting filled with male executives (and who could blame her). So before she goes in, she says to herself, *I am universally loved, adored and respected.* It makes us laugh when we talk about it, but it gives her a boost of confidence and puts her in a positive state of mind, and that is all that matters.

This all may sound too simple to be effective, but the only way you will know is by trying it. Find a positive affirmation that works for you – a word or a sentence that puts you in a positive mindset, and is a creation of the life or situation you want right now. Then say it to yourself internally, or say it out loud, write it in on a sticky note and pop it in your notebook, or on your wall/mirror/fridge, to remind you of it. With people I coach, perhaps one of the most notable and fairly immediate changes they tell me about comes from their positive affirmations.

We are affirming all of the time, whether we know it or not. Most of the time that voice in our head is not our best friend, it is our worst enemy, and can be a complete bitch if we are being real. Yes, you know it's true. Seriously, we wouldn't say a fraction of the things we say to ourselves to our friends; they would turn their backs on us in an instant. We can choose our thoughts, so we might as well choose positive thoughts, that will help to create the life we want to live – that just makes plain old sense. Give it a whirl, be persistent and consistent, and you will be pleasantly surprised by the outcome.

So, now that we have the big kicker out of the way, here are a few other key areas to focus on, to keep your stress thoughts at bay:

···· *Breathe*

We have looked at the breath in Chapter 24. So you now know that breathing mindfully is a fundamental way we not only manage our minds, but also manage our bodies and importantly, our nervous systems. As far as stress is concerned, when we breathe deeply, we trigger the relaxation response. Always remember that your breath is the number one tool you have to be calm and peaceful, and free of the gremlins.

Be mindful

So often, when we feel stressed, it is not because of this moment we are in right now, it is because of all of the other moments that have either gone before, or we think will come after this one. When you are fully present, in this moment, your opportunity to think stressful thoughts lessens significantly, as you are here *now*, not worrying about everywhere else you could be. We have looked at this already in the mindfulness chapter, but it bears reminding (as often as required).

Be prepared

Any book or article, that looks at stress management, will tell you that one of the key tools for managing stress is to be prepared. When you look at my old self, the morning panic mostly came from lack of preparation the night before, or from getting up too late, and not helping myself by getting organised. This sounds simple, but the days when I am smooth sailing are largely down to getting my act together in preparation, as well, of course, as using the three other techniques above. Tried but true.

Try some aromatherapy

This is a thought not covered anywhere else in my book, but I swear by it. There are actually now a lot of scientific studies that have proven the benefits of using aromatherapy, particularly in stress management. My friends know that I am usually bathed in oils. The one I use the most is good old lavender, a gift from the heavens when I need to breathe in peace and happiness, not just say it. There are so many oils available, and they all have different uses. So check them out, see an aromatherapist, or get some lavender oil and see what works for you. It is a little left field for some people, but it works like magic for me, and many people I know. Oh, careful if you are pregnant though – check with a qualified person, before lathering yourself up.

Stress is a scary green monster that can live in the cupboard of our minds and souls and eat away at our very existence. It is that bad. But it doesn't have to be. Throughout this section of the book we are looking at many wellbeing tools and techniques, that will help you to calm the monkey mind, be mindful, breathe for your life, and live a whole, well life. These will all help you learn that, really, there is no stress, only stressful thoughts, and you really are the driver. How empowering is that.

Getting real – *try this*

···• Watch your language. That voice inside your head, that continuously and relentlessly tells you that you are stressed, is unhelpful at best, and completely derailing at worst. Become aware of your language, in your head and in what you say, and learn to choose positive words. Activate your power thoughts, and watch your outlook change, along with your inner dialogue.

···• Your breath is your best friend, and chief warrior against those stress gremlins. There is little more nourishing than a long inhalation and smooth exhalation, and your nervous system (and all other parts of your body) will thank you for it.

···• Remember that you are in control, even when you don't feel like you have control over anything. You are. And if you don't like the way something is right now, you have the power to change it, no matter what it is. Hopefully, the things we talk about in this book will help you find the right path, to do just that. Just believe that it is possible, and you are already on your way there.

CHAPTER 28

Create some space

If you obey all the rules, you miss all the fun.

– Katherine Hepburn

Many of our lives these days are pretty busy. Okay let's be honest, they are crammed to the rafters and set to explode any minute! We couldn't possibly get more stuffed in there if we tried. Feel familiar? As women, we just seem to be so very busy. A lot of it is very important stuff – career, relationships, kids, bosses, friends, domesticity, exercise – you get the drill. But then there are all of the other things, that the generations before us never had to contend with.

We now have a society that has to be connected with constantly. While we may choose to opt out, it is getting increasingly difficult to run our businesses (and our lives) without modern connectivity – *Facebook, Twitter, LinkedIn, Flickr, iPhones, BlackBerrys* and *iPads*, just to name a few. The pressure to always 'be on', always connected, always trying to be just that little bit better, always trying to just keep up, can be overwhelming. And if we don't plan it differently, any semblance of balance, let alone boundaries, can just seem like a distant dream.

Creating space is like drawing a long, slow, beautiful, nurturing breath. If we don't make a conscious choice to create some space in our lives, then life just becomes one race after the other, with no finish line in sight. We end up frazzled and exhausted with the sheer busy-ness of it all. Or worse. The months roll into years, the years into decades, and we wake up one day thinking, *where did my life go?* Now, you may think that is dramatic, but I have seen it too many times not to take it seriously.

And I have been there too. You have read about the time when I changed my job and my life, as I literally had 'no life'. I had a job, a house and a child. And not only were they not coexisting well together, there was not an ounce of breathing space anywhere to be found. And as I have said, it was not a fun place to be. It was downright making me sick.

Now it doesn't need to be that dramatic. It could be a relatively small space, that you need to create for yourself. It could be space to meditate, to go for a walk, to take a bubble bath once a week and have some time for you. It could be creating space to read a book, learn to paint, do formal study, take a cooking lesson, or do some gardening. Or it could be bigger than that. Maybe you want to write a book. Or find a new career. Find a partner even. Maybe you want to buy a new house, travel overseas, or even change the way your whole life is set up, like I did.

Whatever it is, you need to take the time, thought and effort to create space, for whatever it is you want in your life. Things don't just happen. They don't. You have to make a conscious decision, make a plan, and take action.

Creating space can also be on a physical level – literal space. What does your living space look like? What does it feel like? If it is anything like mine, it can get incredibly crowded and cramped with so much crap that I don't know where anything is, just sure it is under a pile somewhere. Mostly that is a pile of books or magazines, but it could just as easily be mail, clothes, clean washing waiting to be ironed, or the school bags piling up at the front door. The point is, new energy cannot flow into our houses and our lives, if we have so much rubbish clogging the path.

My space is usually pretty good, but at certain times, like now, it needs a major overhaul. If you can relate, then make a plan. This weekend I am going to remove the pile of junk that has accumulated in the hallway, which includes by the way, my old wedding dress that was in storage, my son's old computer waiting to go to charity, a pile of clothes with the same fate, wrapping paper, and even my guitar from when I was 15. Arrrggghhhhh. So this weekend, it is on my list to get rid of it all. Because it is sucking my energy, every time I walk past it.

The other way I created space in my house was to cordon off our tiny third bedroom as a yoga and meditation room. Now there could have been a hundred other uses for this room. However, I wanted to create a space where I knew my son and I could go, sit and meditate, do yoga, practise some Pilates on the reformer (which takes up way too much space I might add), or just sit and read, listen to music and contemplate the universe. I go in there every single day. Some days for a long practice, others just to turn on the Zen music that plays as Luca goes to sleep. It is a sacred space in our house, and I wouldn't change it. As my Mum said one day when she was visiting, *you feel calm just by standing at the doorway*.

This space is really important to me for what it symbolises. Calm. Peace. The fact is that I want to meditate every day, and even when I don't get there, I know my cushion is waiting for me (and calling to me to just come and sit my ass down).

So, where do you feel you need to create some space in your life? Is it personal space, like making room in your schedule for a bubble bath, home-based space like removing the clutter, or a big, audacious space you need to clear, for a new life that is waiting for you? I invite you to spend some time to gain clarity on that, and then once you have, make a plan. Take action. And create that space. It might just help you to breathe again.

Getting real – *remember*

···• We all need space in our lives, no matter how busy we are. In fact, the busier we are, the more conscious we need to be about the space we are creating for ourselves.

···• Identify what your needs are, and how you can create the space to fulfil those needs. Be honest with yourself.

···• Remember that you are worth it. Sometimes we feel that we are not worthy, that all of the other things are more important, or that it's just not possible. It is, and you are. So do it now.

CHAPTER 29

Energy is your currency, so manage it

The ultimate measure of our lives is not how much time we spend on the planet, but rather how much energy we invest in the time that we have.

– Tony Schwartz

I n an earlier chapter, we talked about time management, which we know is a key part of productivity. We all need to know how to get the most from our days, and how to manage our time in a way that helps us to be effective and efficient. Rarely can you live an extraordinary life and attain all of your goals, if you do not master how to best use the hours you have in your days.

But there is another important discussion that we need to have, if you really want to live a purposeful and passionate life. That topic is energy. Energy is the new currency. We can talk about time management all we want, but everyone who has ever lived, has had exactly the same number of hours in the day. Energy, on the other hand, is a totally different ball game. How we manage our energy determines not only the quantity we have available to play with, but also the quality of every part of our lives, from our relationships, to our health, to our mental and physical wellbeing, and to our careers.

What I see, from the many women I come into contact with, is that we are in what feels like a permanent energy crisis. As I have talked about so often in this book, we are constantly running, with so much to do and achieve, that we barely have time to stop and breathe before we are off again. What suffers most noticeably, is the quality and quantity of our energy, which impacts on everything we do. And, it impacts on who we are, on the inside and out.

Managing your energy is about many things. It is, of course, about your physical energy; but it is also about your emotional energy, your spiritual energy and your mental energy. I have always believed that we need to look at energy holistically, so I was thrilled to find that there had been a book written, that married up with my philosophies, articulated them and so much more. A few years ago, when I was doing some research for a leadership program I was developing, I stumbled across what is now one of my favourite books, *The Power of Full Engagement*. Tony Schwartz and Jim Loehr talk about the power of energy in great detail, based on their pioneering work in high performance management with elite athletes, and the transference of this work to what they call the 'corporate athlete'.

This book has become a key input into my theories around effective energy management. I truly believe that, if you want to live an extraordinary life, live on purpose, and achieve all you want – or even if you just want to find some balance in your crazy world – then you need to get smart about how you manage your energy (oh, and how you manage everyone's around you too – but we will get to that shortly).

In my book, many of the topics will help you directly with the energy you have, how you create it, and how you manage it, to create the best life possible. In fact, when it comes down to it, it's all about energy. Everything actually is energy – but don't get me started on physics. What we will look at here are a few key points, that I believe are critical and fundamental to getting the most from your energy, and having all that you need to bounce through your days and nights and be the best you can be – sounds good, right? You bet it does. So let's look at some of the key areas of energy, and what you can do to create it, harness it and manage it, to get your sparkle on.

···• Get real about your energy

Firstly, you need to learn to tune in to your energy levels, and understand where your energy is coming from on all levels. So many of us, myself included, sometimes just run and run and run without pause, and then wonder why we find it hard to get out of bed in the morning. We often don't think about our energy until we are at the point of exhaustion, where we need to sleep until noon every Sunday, we are screaming at everyone we know for no reason, or we just burn out. But it doesn't have to be that way. The first step in managing your energy is to acknowledge where you are at, and respect it.

For instance, if you know you are exhausted physically, and have little left in the tank, then act accordingly. I was intending to go to a power yoga class at 7.30am this morning – full on, dynamic flow yoga in a hot room. But when I woke up, I felt really tired, more than usual – you know, that tired-to-your-bones kind of tired. Now, in years gone by, I would have just pushed through and done the class anyway. I would have burned through massive amounts of adrenaline to get through it, and would have come out feeling an initial high of feel-good hormones (maybe) and then crashed and burned soon after. I would have done this, because back then I didn't know any better. But thankfully, I do now. Now I listen to my body and treat it with the respect it deserves. If I need to take a nap, I take one (as often as possible, actually). If I need to go meditate, I do it. If I just need to sit quietly in the corner and breathe, I do that too. Whatever it takes.

And you need to tune in spiritually, emotionally and mentally as well. Some days you have the emotional energy to speak to that friend who always has the husband dramas, and tells you every little detail (for hours on end, bless her), and some days you don't. Some days you can tackle that really complex business issue that your boss wants a report on, and some times you need to leave it to the morning (if you can). And some days, you have nothing left in your little old spiritual self to deal with anything but a bubble bath. It happens. The key is to know how you are feeling on all of these levels energetically, and treat yourself with the same love and kindness that you would give to your best friend.

···• **Program your work and rest cycles**

Pioneering sleep researcher, Nathaniel Kleitman, discovered more than 50 years ago something he called the 'basic rest-activity cycle', which are the 90-minute periods at night when we move through the five stages of sleep. (We will get to this soon in Chapter 33.) What he also discovered is that our bodies operate in the same 90-minute cycles during the day, cycles which other researchers have called the ultradian rhythm.

Most people work for much longer periods than 90 minutes without a break. Think of those all-day management meetings you might attend, or how you work when you have a big report due – you just push through, using your stimulant of choice to keep you going, until you are done. But when we do this, our stress hormones – adrenalin, cortisol and noradrenalin – shift into overdrive to keep us going. We move from our parasympathetic nervous system to our sympathetic one – meaning we have moved into fight or flight mode. And because we are relying on stress hormones for energy, the prefrontal cortex in our brains shuts down, we begin to think less clearly, and we become less effective. Now if all that is a tad scientific for you (or just too much information), then just know this – it is not good, and not a place you want to be for high performance.

The only place you end up, from continued abuse of your body's energy systems, is burnout. And you cannot have sustained success, if you are chronically exhausted. If just doesn't match up. The harder you push and the harder you drive yourself, the more exhausted you get. Take it from someone who has had energy-related, debilitating illnesses (that would be me) – chronic fatigue syndrome, adrenal exhaustion, burn out. Without energy, of all types, there isn't much going on – well, except for recovering – which in itself takes a massive amount of all types of energy. Please trust me when I say that you don't want to go where that path leads.

So the moral of the story is to work along the ultradian rhythm cycle of our bodies, and work in periods of 90 minutes. Then take a short break, to rest and renew our energy resources. This is one of the cornerstones of peak performance management, as outlined by Tony and Jim in their fabulous book. Your rest renewal could be anything – take a shower (unless you are in the board meeting of course), get a cup of tea, take a meditation break, chat to a friend, go for a walk. And it doesn't have to be long either. Ten minutes is enough to restore your resources, but take longer if you have the time available to you.

···• Create energy rituals

What I have learnt from highly successful people, and from the best performance coaches in the world, is that having highly specific energy rituals – essentially, the way you plan your day to fuel your energy – is one of the key criteria for success. And they are planned – they don't just happen.

So, what could this look like? It might mean getting up at 5am to have time to meditate, go for a run, journal or write, before the house wakes up. It might mean building in energy breaks throughout your day, so you are restoring your energy as you move through your work. It might mean what you do in between finishing work and getting home, so you arrive fresh and ready to spend time with the family, instead of tired, grumpy and wanting a bottle of vodka.

We talk about creating positive rituals in Chapter 35 of this book, so start thinking about what your energy rituals could look like, and then you will have the chance to create them later. They are incredibly important, and they might just be the keys to your success.

···· The energy you bring

When you think about energy, it's also important to realise that it's not all about you – sorry to break it to you. You know those people who storm into a room, huffing and puffing, creating chaos and inflicting their foul mood onto everyone? Well, they are literally inflicting their energy. Energy, like so many things, is infectious. It's scientifically proven to be contagious. It is really important to think about the energy you bring, wherever you are. Think about it. What energy do you bring, when you walk into work everyday? A team at a place where I have worked said that they all used to sit and wait with bated breath until the boss walked in everyday, as they knew what their day would look like by how he walked the floor in the morning. If he was tense or frustrated, they knew they were in for a piece of hell. If he was happy and joking around with everyone, they breathed easy.

Your energy matters. How you show up matters. Dr Jill Bolte Taylor is a Harvard-trained neuroanatomist – a scientist who specialises in how the brain works. She is also the author of the book *My stroke of insight*. She had a massive, rare type of stroke, which took her eight years to recover from. In a great interview by Dr Mehmet Oz (on www.Oprah.com), Jill says the energy of the people around her played an important role in her recovery. *Take responsibility for the energy you bring*, she says. Jill says she could feel the energy of the people who walked in her room, and could even tell which nurses made her feel safe. The nurses who would make a connection with her, simply by making eye contact or touching her foot, made all the difference. *As opposed to someone who just comes in, deals with the machinery, ignores that there's even a warm body in the bed*, she says. *I didn't feel safe in that person's care.*

This is a beautiful illustration of just how palpable your energy is, the impact you have on other people, and how important it is to be conscious of it.

Energy. It's not something many people think about, until they don't have any. Actually it's much like the electricity in our homes – you don't worry about it until the light doesn't go on (or you get the bill, which is a useful analogy in itself). Whether it is physical, emotional, spiritual or mental, we all can do a better job of creating, harnessing and managing our energy sources. It is a fundamental key to both high performance and happiness, and to becoming the well woman you know you deserve to be.

Getting real – *remember*

····• Energy is the new currency. We all have the same amount of hours in the day, but the amount of energy we have is entirely up to us.

····• Tune in to your energy, and get real about where you are at – on a body, mind and spirit level – and manage yourself accordingly.

····• Plan rituals to create your energy, work in 90-minute cycles to harness it, and be conscious of the energy you bring into a room. You may not be able to see it, but those around you can certainly feel it. So make sure you are bringing the best, most positive energy possible with you, whenever possible.

CHAPTER 30

Nourish your body

Take care of your body. It's the only place you have to live.

– Jim Rohn

ood. Nutrition. Nourishment. Not words that always go together for many people. Food. Guilt. Confusion. Stress. They are words that often go together for too many people! So many women I know have baggage, issues or challenges around food (or all of the above). We eat too much. We don't eat enough. We eat too much crap. We don't know what to eat at all. Oh, my lordy lord, when did it all get so hard? And when did so much guilt and angst get thrown in to the mix, with something that used to be so very simple?

Well, I want to make this as simple as humanly possible. I am not going to be prescriptive and tell you exactly what to eat, how much to eat, when to eat, and how to eat a pineapple while standing on your head. There are plenty of resources out there that can do that (well, except for the pineapple thing, I just made that up). What I want to do is share some very simple philosophies on food that I believe in. I hope they will shed some light and plant some seeds on how you can truly nourish yourself, through the choices you make about what you put in your body.

There are so many perspectives out there about everything to do with food. Food is a squillion dollar industry. There are so many people and organisations interested in what you eat and how they can make money from it – no wonder we are so confused about what is good for us. High fat, low fat, no fat; low carb, high protein, no sugar; Atkins, South Beach, Paleo; raw, vegan, vegetarian – the lists are literally endless. Everyone has an opinion, and everyone is pushing something. It's time to get back to basics.

In his best-selling book, *In Defense of Food*, Michael Pollan said, *Eat food, not too much, mostly plants.* As far as my views on nutrition and nourishment go, this pretty much sums it up, and we will look at why in this chapter. And as I said, I want to keep it simple.

So what is my personal opinion about nourishment and how can it help you? Well, I am so pleased you asked. I offer here some kind advice – not rules, not directives – just gentle guidance. It may give you some food for thought (pun intended) about what you might want to put in your body and why. These are the key principles I live by, and they make a huge difference to my life, my health, and how I feel about myself, when I do them well (which is not always I might add; you know by now that I have a slight cupcake addiction, but I do my best).

···• Drink something green every day

I am a huge fan of green smoothies and green juices. Smoothies are essential for me, as they give me a huge dose of goodness and they are quick and easy. I can whip one up and drink it in about five minutes. I recommend you get yourself the best blender and juicer you can afford. I use the Vita Mix blender, and I have a great, powerful juicer. They are a really good investment, and will make a massive difference to your health. My go-to green smoothie looks something like this:

···• *Megan's Green Smoothie*
All organic ingredients where possible

Around 150ml filtered water
One cucumber
One green apple
Big bunch of spinach
Some celery stalks
Big handful of mint
Some ice cubes

It's super simple and delicious. If you are starting out, use baby spinach, as it has such a subtle taste you won't even realise you are drinking it. On a good day, I can even get my son to drink a glass, and that is saying something. The mint masks the green flavor, which helps as you ease into green drinks. After a while, you will actually crave the taste – trust me it's true, even if it's hard to believe now. You can throw in whatever greens you have in your fridge and experiment with the taste, to get to something you love. I crave this when I am travelling and can't have it every day.

When juicing and blending, try to stay away from too much fruit. Go big on the leafy greens and super foods like cucumber. Juicing fruit can mean that what you are really getting is a big glass of sugar, as fruit has high sugar content. So be careful. It's goodness, but a little goes a long way. On the other hand, you would be hard-pressed to drink too many green vegies. Try them; your skin, your body, your energy and vitality will all show a massive improvement. It's the fastest way to get your glow on.

A side note: as well as drinking a big glass of green goodness every day, you might also want to also consider how much other green stuff is in your diet. If you had a green smoothie for breakfast, a big salad for lunch, more salad and leafy greens with your protein meal for dinner (meat, chicken, fish, quinoa, tofu!) you would be well on your way to having a massive dose of healthy nutrients to keep you energised all day. Not only that, the green stuff alkalises your body, as opposed to keeping it acidic, which can help to ward off illness, disease and other murky stuff that you don't want anywhere near your body. Get conscious about where the greens are showing up on your plate – you may find when you start to look for them, that they are nowhere to be found. Get them in your diet, at every meal, and you will see a world of difference in your body (and in your mind and spirit too).

···• Get off the white stuff

No, not the crack, the sugar – well actually, it is pretty much the same thing to your body. They are both crazily addictive and drive your brain and body insane, so the sugar has to go. You knew this one was coming, so brace yourself. Back in the golden days (think when we were little girls in pigtails), sugar was a sacred treat reserved for special occasions or when we were 'good girls'. Now, it is in nearly every processed food we eat. Check the labels on your next trip to the supermarket and you will see what I mean. It is in everything, and has many disguises.

Let's look at some of the things this horrid substance does to you. It causes inflammation in your cells, strips minerals from your body, feeds candida, fuels osteoporosis, diabetes and cancer, stresses your nervous system, exhausts your adrenals, and messes with your hormones. It wreaks havoc on your immune system, your emotions, and your self-control. It is also chronically addictive because, for a short period of time, it makes us feel good. It gives us a boost of dopamine, the feel-good hormone and therefore, not surprisingly, we crave more of it. And here is the crack part – we know from research that the cycle of craving, withdrawal and relapse, that we experience as a sugar addict, is an eerily similar cycle to the one that heroin and cocaine users go through. So it's serious stuff we are talking about.

I could go on and on and on about this, but I am sure you get the picture. I know it's not easy, and is arguably one of the hardest healthy habits to stick to. It's my addiction of choice, so I have lived through the process of kicking it many times. But it's worth persevering, and you will really feel a whole lot different and better when you do.

Oh, and while we are on the white stuff – get off all the other white stuff too. White processed grains like white bread, white rice, and anything with white flour in it, are not the best choices you can make. Go for whole foods and whole grains wherever you can, and kick the white stuff out of your diet.

···• Go organic wherever possible

There is still so much discussion about whether it is worth it to go organic. No matter what study I look at, and I have looked at many, I read that, on average, organic produce has remarkably more nutrients than non-organic foods. As my friend, leading food philosopher and nutritionist Sherry Strong says, *Studies on organic food, independent of the food industry, show a 40 to 60 percent increase in nutrients in organic foods, which means you get more bang for your buck, along with knowing that toxic and carcinogenic chemicals are not used on your food. But not all organic foods are healthy – sugary cereals, ice cream, chocolate bars that are certified organic are not health foods, they are simply luxury foods that have less damaging chemicals in them.*

While we are talking pure, drink pure water as well. Even though there is still great debate about what is actually in our tap water and what it does to our bodies, you know that the water that comes from a pure spring has to be better for us than water through rusty pipes, potentially filled with yucky stuff. But don't just take my word for it – listen to Sherry: *It is one of the most important things you will do for your health. So-called experts are telling us how healthy tap water is. The problem is that water companies hire many of the experts quoted, and independent experts have differing views. Sadly, tap water is both fluoridated and chlorinated in most cities, certainly in Australia. I recommend highly to source water from a spring that is regularly tested, or get a really good water filter.*

So where you can, buy organic and drink pure. They are two of the simplest food rules I live by.

···· Go light in the evening

Many of us in western cultures have been brought up not paying too much attention to what we eat during the day – sometimes even missing meals as we are too busy. Then we sit down for a 'proper' meal in the evening, eating everything in sight, as we are literally starved of nutrients and sustenance. Sound familiar? Many people also comfort eat in the evening, to fill a hunger that is really not about food at all; it's about tiredness, loneliness, stress, anxiety or boredom, just to name a few. I have a card on my Pinterest 'Fitness Inspiration' board, which says: *You're not hungry, you're bored. Learn the difference.* So many of us find it very challenging to do this (psst, the chapters on mindfulness, breathing and meditation are keys here, so check them out again if this one is an issue for you – and don't feel bad, it is for me too).

The problem with eating large meals in the evening, unless you are an athlete and then go and train for two hours, is that our bodies have to spend the night trying to digest that food, instead of doing what they are meant to be doing, which is restoring and healing our systems while we sleep. A much better use of our time. So go easy and light on the dinner in the evening, and see what difference it makes for you. Experiment with what 'light' means for you. For me it means soup, or a salad, some sushi, perhaps fish and salad or vegies, and maybe followed by a small piece of dark chocolate. Now this isn't every night of course. The nights I go out for dinner I will eat heavier than that, and there are the nights when I want to scoff everything in sight. I told you at the start that I was far from perfect. But most nights, I go light, sleep well, and feel better for it the next day. Try it out for yourself.

Listen to your body

You know by now how big I am on mindfulness, and how living consciously is the most effective way to be in the world. When it comes to food, listening to your body through being mindful about when you are hungry, what you are hungry for, and what your body needs, are critical ingredients to health and happiness through nourishment. I asked Sherry about the best way to get in touch with your body, so you know what it really needs. No surprises with her answer: *You need to slow down. Observe what you are eating and how it affects your body. It sounds simple and impossible for many people, but it is the only way. Moving away from processed foods and incorporating whole, unprocessed, seasonal, local organic foods will change your life.*

Limit caffeine

I haven't been able to drink caffeine for over a decade, due to my arrhythmia (chronic heart palpations brought on by stimulants, stress and other stuff – nasty). And while that was once quite devastating for me, as coffee is one of my favourite things (I still drink a mean decaf), I believe I developed this heart condition as a way of my body telling me to slow the hell down (insert other word for more impact). I used to drink three or more large double coffees every day, run on little sleep, and use this stimulant and others to fuel my obsession with working 16-hour days. Your body can only run on fake sources of energy for so long, before it tells you to go and take a hike.

Now I am not saying that you should never drink coffee. I know it is one of life's great pleasures for many people. And there is a lot of research that spells out the benefits of good quality coffee (and tea), when drunk in moderation. But be careful. Using any form of caffeine, as a crutch to get you through the day, can be a recipe for disaster. If you are tired, then you need to know that you are tired and deal with the root cause. Of course, there are times when we all just need to soldier on. But when you continually run on the adrenaline that caffeine feeds, you can end up burning out your adrenals and getting in to a whole word of hurt.

Start to notice how you feel when you only have one coffee hit per day. What other tips and tools from this book can you use to build your natural energy resources – have a green juice, meditate, do some exercise, get more sleep. But don't be a caffeine junkie. It may serve you in the short term, but it will kick your ass in the long run.

So there you have it. A few simple rules that I endeavour to live by. I hope you have found something here that will stimulate you to look at how you nourish yourself. It is one of the most critical things we can do, when we are thinking about getting real, and being well.

Getting real – *remember*

····• What you put in your body has a massive impact on how you feel, how you perform, and the energy you bring to your life.

····• Choose wisely. Eat organic, drink pure water, limit your caffeine, eat lightly when the sun goes down, and don't forget to get your green on! These are simple, easy to live by philosophies, that will change how you feel inside your skin.

····• Want more? Check out my website for a heap of cool books from my health gurus, links to Sherry's websites, as well as some of my kitchen spun recipes on my blog that you can delve into, to feed your passion for nourishing your body. Enjoy!

CHAPTER 31

Get moving and get your yoga on

I have to exercise in the morning
before my brain figures out what I'm doing.

– Marsha Doble

A few years ago, I lived on the beach for two years. I had just come out of a heart-wrenching break up, and the beach turned out to be my greatest refuge. Every day, I would wake up listening to the waves, and at night I would meditate and go to sleep hearing the ocean, lulling me to a peaceful sleep. In between, I would exercise (when I wasn't working, raising my son, studying, and all that other stuff, naturally). Each morning when I was working from home, I would take a long fast walk on the beach, usually on the soft sand. I would then have a beautiful swim in the sea, swimming laps, treading water, and eventually floating on my back, carried by the gentle waves, feeling peaceful after my work-out. On the days when I was in the office, I would get home, change, and get out and do the same thing, most days with Luca. Other days we would ride our bikes along the esplanade, and then come back and hit the water. And anytime I could in between, I was doing yoga (more on that later).

Sounds good, right? It was utter bliss. Exercise was a huge part of my healing process. I was in the best shape I had been in years, and my spirit and zest returned over the course of that first year at the beach.

Compare this to last year. For a period of six months last year, while working my corporate job, being a single parent, and developing the *World Wellness Project*, I was also completing the final year of my (second) masters degree, in Wellness no less, and writing my thesis on Positive Leadership. You could say I was pretty busy. Other than the odd walk and yoga class, I really didn't exercise. I felt like crap most of the time, I lost all of my hard-earned fitness, and, you guessed it, I put on ten kilos. Holy crap is right! Frustrating didn't begin to cover it because, of course, I should have known better. And my lack of exercise had flow-on effects into the other healthy habits that I had spent years crafting for myself: my meditation practice slipped, my bedtime ritual gave way to long nights at the computer researching and writing, and my healthy eating habits pretty much went out the window. I succumbed to the pressure of my work and looming deadlines, and to the stress of my life. Not a pretty picture. And I know that if I had just done one thing, kept up my exercise routine, doing something every day like I had for so many years, that none of this would have happened, and I would have managed myself, my thesis and my life much better. The joy of hindsight I know.

Exercise. We all know we need to do it. We all know that we need both cardiovascular exercise and strength training to be fit and strong, look after our hearts and also our bones. We know this, right? I see you nodding, so in this chapter I won't belabour the basic fundamentals of why we need to move our butts. You can see, from my own life experience, what happens when we do, and when we don't. And I am sure you have your own experience as well. What I want to do in this chapter, is point out some of the lesser-known reasons why it pays to get your feet into your running shoes. And I want to spend a chunk of this chapter on yoga, to highlight the squillions of benefits and hopefully, for you non-yogis out there, get you on the mat.

···· **Why exercise?**

Okay, so we know that exercise makes us healthier, by increasing our cardiovascular fitness, improving our strength and keeping us agile. But here are some interesting reasons you may not be aware of, that are just as important to our general wellbeing and success:

···· *Exercise kicks your brain up a notch*

While we once thought that the brain had finite growth potential, neuroscientists have recently found that exercise actually promotes the growth of your brain. For those detailed nuts among you, it specifically hits a molecule known as Brain Derived Neurotrophic Growth Factor or BDNF (say what?). The impact is that you are more ready, willing and able to learn. Exercisers do much better than their couch potato friends in tests that measure long-term memory, reasoning, attention and problem solving. Physical activity is cognitive candy for the brain. Yum!

···· *Exercise makes you more productive at work*

The *Journal of Occupational and Environmental Medicine* reported on research conducted in a Swedish organisation. The research had one group with a 2.5-hour per week exercise program during work hours, and another group had the same 2.5-hour reduction in work, but no exercise. A third group worked the same hours and had no exercise program. The research found that the group that participated in the exercise program not only felt 'more productive' but also had less sick days. Makes sense then, that getting in your exercise is good for your career, as well as your body.

···· *Exercise can help that bad temper*

Well I sure know someone who could use that bit of knowledge! Research reported in the *New York Times* recently, by stress physiologist Nathaniel Thom, says that even a single bout of exercise can have a robust prophylactic effect against the build up of anger. He says, *it's like taking an aspirin to combat heart disease, you reduce your risk.* He also says, *If you know that you're going to be entering into a situation that is likely to make you angry, go for a run first.* Good advice to go break a sweat, however you want to do it.

···• *Exercise is like a magic drug for depression and anxiety*
Many of us get anxious at times, I know I do, and the statistics on the rise of depression are out of control. We know that getting your work-out done boosts serotonin levels, the happy hormone. But scientists at Southern Methodist University and Boston University are discovering that the benefits are more powerful than we ever realised. Michael Otto, psychology professor at BU, says, *Exercise appears to affect, like an antidepressant, particular neurotransmitter systems in the brain, and it helps patients with depression re-establish positive behaviours. For patients with anxiety disorders, exercise reduces their fears and related bodily sensations such as a racing heart and rapid breathing.* And just 25 minutes is enough for the effects to kick in, and make the difference between a good day and a bad one. So get moving!

So there you have it. There are so many reasons to move your butt, and no legitimate ones not to – it's pretty simple really.

···• **Get your yoga on**
Now, let's look at my all-time favourite exercise, yoga. Actually, when I think about it, I don't consider it exercise – even when I am sweating my ass off in a hot room with my body contorted into all sorts of crazy positions. I call it my soul food.

Yoga is about more than just moving your body. Sure, yoga is great for strengthening, stretching and improving your fitness; but it is so much more than that. Originating in ancient India many lifetimes ago (2nd century BC to be exact), yoga is a physical, mental and spiritual discipline that can inspire peace and tranquility, bring you in touch with your body and quieten your mind. In fact the word 'yoga' means union in Sanskrit, and the ultimate goal is to achieve moksha – no, not a fancy name for a hybrid coffee drink – but liberation from all worldly suffering. Gee, not bad for just getting yourself on your yoga mat, right? Well, it takes a little bit of work to get there, like a lifetime, but the fun is in the journey.

Yoga takes many forms, from the ancient traditional hatha practice, to styles like Bikram yoga (hot – like really really really hot), Yin yoga (more restorative), Power yoga (dynamic flowing yoga) and literally dozens of others. The key is to find the yoga that fits for you.

I started attending classes a few decades ago, as something told me that I would love it and that it would be a wonderful practice for me. It took quite a few years for us to click though – yoga and me. I tried Iyengar, which is very structured with the use of props like blocks and straps, and focuses on proper alignment. I found this a little too structured for me (reminiscent of ballet practice and strict adherence to positions – and the odd shoe being flung at me for getting it wrong – didn't want to go back there!). I tried full-on classes like Bikram, in a very hot room. While I loved Bikram, my body didn't like it so much, as the heat was a little overwhelming for me to do three times a week, although I still do it occasionally.

And then I found globally-renowned author and teacher, Christina Brown. I stumbled across Christina when she owned *Life Source* in Sydney, took her Friday lunchtime class one day, and fell in love. She is an amazing and inspirational teacher who made yoga fun, holding it lightly and taking her students on a journey of discovery. I loved her classes so much, that I decided a few years later to do my yoga teacher training with her, which was one of the best years of my life (coincidently, it was also the same year that I started living on the beach, as I talked about earlier in this chapter – again, part of my year of self-discovery and healing).

I also love teaching yoga. I can't describe the feeling of seeing students walk in at the beginning of class, stressed, rushed, cranky and over it, transformed at the end of class to a state of utter relaxation and bliss. It's hard to beat, and such a gift, to be able to guide someone along that path to peace and tranquility.

I encourage you to discover a yoga practice that is all yours, or deepen your practice if you already have one. It can take a while to click with a certain style, find the right teacher, or discover the yoga studio that inspires you and makes you feel at home. Or sometimes you just fall into it with grace and ease. Whichever way you come to yoga, it's worth the process of discovery to find what is right for you. It is a journey of awakening. Whether you want to do it for the calming effects, to get that enviable yoga body, to ease your busy mind, or to make new friends, it is a journey that can be life-changing. It certainly has been for me.

Getting real – *remember*

···• Always check with your doctor or health care practitioner before starting any form of exercise program. I know, I know, you hear that all the time. But it's important, especially if you have been inactive for a while.

···• Find the type of exercise that you love and look forward to. There is absolutely no point doing something you hate and that you dread. You will not be consistent, and your body, mind and spirit will not be the better for it. Find something you can get excited about.

···• On those days when you just don't want to do anything (yep, I have them, don't you worry), just commit to doing ten minutes. Most times, after a short period, your endorphins will kick in and you will be off and running. If after ten minutes you're really tired and not feeling it, give it a rest for the day and pick it up again tomorrow.

CHAPTER 32

Restore yourself

There must be quite a few things in life that a hot bath
won't cure, but I don't know many of them.

– Sylvia Plath

I picked up a new tea last week. For those who know me, this would come as no surprise, as I am a bit of a tea junkie, with at least 30 different herbal blends in my cupboards. This new one is called *Go-Go*, with the tag line being *When your up and go has gone*. How great is that. I had to buy it for the label alone (and the blend is spearmint, peppermint and liquorice for those who want to know, and I am drinking it right now).

Who doesn't feel like that at times, like your up and go has just up and left? I do, and I am yet to meet someone who doesn't. We all have times when we just want to stay in bed, curl up on the couch and watch a movie, or just sit idly and do nothing. I slept in and lay in bed on Sunday until after noon. Noon. I know! Complete luxury that might happen once every six months, with the schedule I keep. But I needed it. I was exhausted. So, instead of getting up at 7am to write, then going for an hour's walk, doing some yoga, and writing for the rest of the day, I stayed in bed, then had a shower, went to my favourite café to get some yummy food, and spent the best part of the afternoon in my favourite lounge chair watching movies. I needed some downtime, to restore myself, give my brain a break, and just do nothing. And I have to tell you, I felt like a different person on Monday when I went to the office. How often do you just stop, rest, and give yourself a break, to truly restore your system?

Restore yourself. Nurture yourself. Look after yourself. Take your pick. They are all talking about the same thing. I hate to say it, but it is one of the things that women generally do really badly – sorry ladies, but you know it's true. If I were to ask you, what you have done in the past week to really nurture yourself, what would you say? For many women I know, they would stare blankly at me, as if I have two heads, pink hair and am speaking to them from the planet Mars.

We are all so very busy. Ridiculously, crazily, out-of-our-minds busy. We have talked about that a lot throughout this book. As women, we do talk about that a lot. But what we don't talk about very much is how we refuel our bodies, minds and spirits, so we can thrive, not just exist.

It took me a very long time to understand this topic – decades in fact. And to this day, it still goes against my inherent need and desire to strive. As you well know by now, from the personal stories I have shared throughout this book, I have been good at many things in my life. But looking after myself, until the last few years, has not been one of them. However, one of the most important things I have learnt on my journey, and perhaps the thing that has lead me to where I am now more than anything else, has been learning about restoration. And if I only give you one gift of knowledge and insight through this entire book, then learning how to nurture yourself, and restore you body, mind and spirit, would be the gift I would want to bestow on you.

When I began my wellness journey, through my yoga teacher training, and then my Master of Wellness degree, I know what I was really yearning for was to feel restored. I wanted to learn how to feel well. I had been running on empty for so many years. Even though this state was second nature to me, I knew somewhere deep down in my soul, that there was something else. A place of peace, of true wellbeing, of deep calm, and the only way I could get to that place, was to stop, and to restore myself.

So what do I mean by restore? I mean doing things that leave you feeling well, rested, cared for and peaceful. I know it may seem like a ridiculously big hill to climb from where you may be currently sitting. But it is not that far a stretch, if you have a tool kit of restorative practices to draw from. I love rescue remedy, which you may have tried. They call it yoga in a bottle and it absolutely is that for me – flower essences that calm through a few drops on the tongue – pure magic. Well, for restoration, I have what I like to call my 'restore me' tool kit, and I have a bag full of stuff that I can draw from, when I feel I need a restoration rescue.

My kit includes things like:

···• a bubble bath with lavender essential oils (and lots of bubbles)

···• meditation – even five minutes can sort me out

···• sitting quietly with my breath

···• inhaling some calming or grounding aromatherapy oils. Some of my favourites for this purpose are sandalwood, frankincense, and my all-time favourite, lavender – I usually have a bottle with me wherever I go, and they are scattered all over my house

···• restorative yoga poses, especially *Legs Up The Wall* (no that's not the technical term. The Sanskrit is *Viparita Kirani*, check out my website)

···• a walk outside

···• sitting by the ocean or under a tree – getting in touch with nature and lapping up some sunshine

···• sleep – it cannot be overstated how important this is (see sleep chapter)

····• reading something inspiring or nurturing

····• looking at my vision wall (or my latest obsession, *Pinterest* vision boards)

····• phoning a friend or my Mum

····• having a nice calming cup of tea

Each one of these, used at different times, picks me up, calms me down and gives me back my energy. Your list could look really different to mine, and different to your best friend or your work colleague. That's great – the important thing is to build a list that works for you.

While I casually refer to this as my rescue kit, it is so important that we don't just do something restorative for ourselves when we are on the brink of collapse. We need to build small restoring rituals into the course of our day, every day, to continually replenish our energy. The more we do this, the less chance we have of getting to the point where you feel like the walls are closing in and you just need to sleep for a month. Oh yes, I have been there – believe me. Rituals look different for everyone. It could be you build in a meditation break for 15 minutes every afternoon, it could be taking a walk midmorning, listening to some music while eating your lunch, or reading some pages from a book after dinner. Or it could be my all-time favourite, the afternoon 30-minute nap. Nothing feels quite as decadent and peaceful to me, as climbing under the covers for a short nap break in the middle of the afternoon. But be careful – no more than 30 minutes, or you won't want to get up and may just stay there until morning.

Oh, and a word to the wise – and those TV watchers among you (I am one too, don't worry). While we may think that plopping down in front of the TV each night is restorative, because we are 'relaxing', be careful. This form of passive leisure is enjoyable for around 30 minutes. But researcher Shawn Achor, author of *The*

Happiness Advantage, tells us that any more time than this, and your energy begins to get sapped, making you feel worse than you did before, because your dopamine levels have taken a dive. This can leave you feeling moody, grumpy and even more tired. Now I am with you – it is not unusual for me to plop down in my cosy chair in front of my TV after a long day, to watch whatever version of *The Real Housewives of New York* (or Beverly Hills) happens to be on. Yes, I admit it, I am a closet reality TV watcher – who would have thought (and don't even get me started on *The West Wing* or I can lose an entire day). But I know that I can only take a short dose before I feel the sleepiness hit come on. So I now limit my TV consumption, and do something that I know will really restore me, like the things on my list. Experiment with it for yourself, and you will see what I mean.

Restoration. It's about balancing out our energy, especially the frenetic, please everyone, do everything, get it all done type energy that many of us live our lives surviving in. But I know there is a different way, and I want you to know it too. There is a better way of being in the world. A kinder and gentler way. And even those among you who say you are fine just the way you are, running on empty, I can promise you that our lifestyles catch up with us eventually, and they usually kick us in the butt when we least expect it. So have a play with these ideas, take a few things out for a spin, and see how you feel. Work out what is best for you, what makes you feel your best, truly restored, and ensure you do it. You will feel all shiny and new.

Getting real – *remember*

···• Create a personal 'restore me' kit that incudes things you love – things that nurture you and bring you back to your equilibrium.

···• Make a commitment to do something restorative for yourself every day – yes, you heard me right – every day.

···• Get to know yourself, so you know those times when you need a little extra nurturing – you now have the tools to draw from to really look after yourself during those times of need. Your body, mind, spirit, and those around you, will thank you for it.

CHAPTER 33

Love your sleep

Sleep is the best meditation.

– The Dalai Lama

In this chapter, we are going to look at whether you are getting enough on a regular basis. Sleep that is – what were you thinking about? So how was your sleep last night? Did you get to bed before 10pm, in a darkened room, and sleep without waking for eight blissful hours? Did you wake refreshed, energised, and leap out of bed this morning, ready to take on the world? No? Really? Welcome to the very large club of women, who very rarely experience this. No matter how tired we are, sometimes it is just impossible to get the sleep we need. And ironically, the more tired we are, the harder it can become. Well, right here we are going to try and put an end to that dilemma. We are goddesses, and goddesses need their sleep, God damn it! So bring your fine, potentially sleep-deprived self with me, and let's take a journey into sleep wonderland. We will look here at how much we really need, why we need it, and importantly, how to get it.

···• How much do we really need, and why?

So let's start with the why. Why do we need so much sleep anyway? We have so much to do, surely squeezing in five hours a night is fine, right? Wrong. Lack of consistent, adequate sleep has been linked to many health issues: from heart disease, to diabetes, from weight gain and cancer, to Alzheimer's.

Firstly, it's really important to understand the sleep cycle. We know from research that not all sleep is created equal. If you think that the quality of your sleep from 1am to 9am is the same as your sleep from 10pm to 6am, you would be wrong again – sorry.

When we sleep, we follow the four cycles of the sleep-wake cycle, and each stage is very different. Each cycle is vital for both your body and mind, and they each play a different role in getting you ready for the next day. Here are the four sleep cycles:

Stage One – Transition to sleep: this can last from five to 15 minutes in most people, and is where we are generally getting ready to sleep.

Stage Two – Light sleep: our first stage of real sleep, this usually lasts from around ten to 30 minutes and is where our heart rate slows down, our body temperature drops and our eye movement stops. Off to slumberland we go.

Stage Three – Deep sleep: we are deep into our blissful state by now. In deep sleep, we are difficult to wake up and disoriented when we do wake. In this state, our brain waves are really slow, blood flow is directed away from our brain to our muscles, and we are busy restoring our physical energy, so we can bounce out of bed in the morning.

Stage Four – REM sleep or dream sleep: once we have been asleep for about 70 to 90 minutes, we enter REM sleep, and dreaming happens here. Our breathing is shallow, heart rate and blood pressure increase and our eyes move back and forth rapidly – which is why this cycle is called Rapid Eye Movement sleep. Makes sense then!

So during the night, sleep goes through a predictable, repeatable pattern, where it cycles through the stages from restorative deep sleep, to alert and dreaming REM sleep, and back again. The cycles typically last around 90 minutes. If you get enough beauty sleep each night, you will repeat the cycle four to six times. The most important sleep is the deep restorative sleep that occurs in Stage Three, and most of this deep sleep occurs in the first half of the night. This is why you will often hear people say that the hours before midnight are the most important to be asleep, and explains the 10pm curfew many sleep experts talk about.

···• How do you now if you are getting enough?

So, just how do you know if you are getting enough sleep? You feel all right most of the time, so there's no issue, right? Well, maybe, but maybe not. Sometimes, you can be so consistently sleep deprived, that you are in what you believe to be your state of normal – you don't even realise how tired you are, as you don't know there is an alternative way to feel. Here are some of the signs that you may be sleep deprived:

···• you need an alarm to get you up

···• you hit the snooze button, maybe even more than once (um, guilty)

···• face it; you just don't want to get your sweet ass out of bed at all

···• you get tired throughout the day, especially in the afternoon

···• you want to put your head on the desk in your meetings, and take a nap right there and then

···• you are desperate to catch up on sleep on the weekend, and sleep in as much as possible

···• you fall asleep within five minutes of getting into bed (bet your partner is particularly happy about that one)

Does any of this sound familiar? It certainly does for me from time to time, no question. Now, of course these things mentioned above can all stem from multiple causes. You have pad thai for lunch, and feel like crawling under your desk straight afterwards to sleep off the carb hit – we know how that one goes. But when you experience these symptoms on an ongoing basis, you really do need to look at your sleeping habits.

It's not just the dark circles under your eyes that need some attention, when you don't get the rest your body needs. There are other prices to pay for not hitting the sack for a solid eight hours every night. Sleep deprivation can cause a lack of motivation, moodiness, inability to cope with stress, reduced immunity, lack of concentration and memory problems, increased risk of accidents, major health problems like heart disease and, wait for it ladies – weight gain. Gasp. I know! If that list isn't enough to motivate you right into the bedroom, I don't know what would. I don't think you need any more prodding. So let's look now at how to make it happen.

···• My tips for getting the best sleep

···• *Shut it all down*

Step away from the computer. And while you're at it, turn off the television, the iPad, iPod, iPhone and anything else that gives off light. Yes, it's sad but true. Using any electronic device up to two hours before bedtime can seriously interfere with your beauty sleep. Once I learnt this, my extremely bad habit of working until late on my laptop, and then getting into bed and checking my emails last minute on my Blackberry, had to go. And here's why. Our sleep-promoting hormone, melatonin, is suppressed by light – any kind of light – but especially the blue waves given off by LEDs (light-emitting diodes, if you really want to know). Much research has been done on this, and the upshot is, that not only will LED light impact you on the night of use, the effect also lingers and can impact your sleep on subsequent nights as well. So, get all those devices and the TV turned off at least 30 to 60 minutes before bed, longer if you are able. You will really notice the difference in your ability to fall asleep, and stay asleep.

···· *While you're at it, cool it down*

To get to sleep, our body temperature needs to cool down from the heat and activity of the day, as our temperature and the brain's sleep-wake cycles are closely tied. Ever tried to fall asleep on a hot summer's night? Not so easy. So cool down, don't pile up with thick blankets if you can help it, and keep some fresh air coming into the room during the night. This will help you nod off into dreamland, and stay there.

···· *Create a bedtime ritual*

One of the most effective ways I have moved from all-night workaholic insomniac to the land of the dreamtime, is my bedtime routine. Creating a bedtime ritual that brings peace, calm and tranquility to your evening is a wonderful way to create a formal break from the busy-ness of the day. It will lead you on a pathway to slumber that is relaxing and sleep inducing. My bedtime ritual goes something like this: once the house is quiet for the night with my son in bed and the last of my work done, I pad my way down to the kitchen. I take my evening vitamins, and make myself a cup of bedtime tea (any form of nighttime, relaxing tea is fine, in a ready-made blend, or good old chamomile is fabulous too). I turn off all the lights and head upstairs. I then usually do some gentle restorative yoga, and then hop into bed with a book or a magazine. Now this is key – I spend heaps of time reading business books, and self-development/ psychology/neuroscience type books that are highly stimulating. My bedtime reading needs to be very light, or it will keep me up all night with new ideas. So I read a chapter of a spiritual book, or flick through a yoga or health mag, and I drink my tea. Then I put a few drops of lavender oil on my temples and it's lights out. I do a ten or so minute meditation while lying in bed, and then it's off to dreamland for me. I have been doing this for so long now it is one of my healthy habits, a ritual I really look forward to, and it is calming for the sheer sense that it is a ritual. When I am travelling like I am at the moment, it also brings a sense of place and grounding to me, and I feel off kilter without doing this before sleep.

Sleep. It can often be the first thing to go, when you are busy. You think you can just get by on those five hours and all will be well. Well, chances are it won't be. You need your sleep for more than your beauty: you need it for your mental, spiritual, physical and emotional wellbeing. And you need it to function well in the world. So make sleep a priority, and see how much better you feel in the morning – and for the rest of your day as well.

Getting real – *remember*

···• Turn off your electronics and television at least 30-60 minutes before bedtime, to give your melatonin a chance to kick in, and help induce sleep.

···• Establish yourself a bedtime routine, to break from the day and bring peace and tranquillity to your bedtime.

···• Give yourself a curfew. 10pm is ideal, and definitely no later than 11pm. Remember that the hours before midnight are worth double the hours after, in terms of sleep quality and benefit.

CHAPTER 34

Take breaks, and take those holidays

Each person deserves a day away in which no problems are confronted, no solutions searched for.

– Maya Angelou

As I write this, I am sitting in a hotel room in New York City, in the middle of a four-week vacation with Luca and my parents. Four-week holiday I hear you scream? Yep, four, long, beautiful, peaceful weeks (well, mostly peaceful – I am with an 11-year-old). Now, before you completely fall off your chair or throw my book at the wall (please don't!), I should tell you that, until a few years ago, I never, ever, took more than a week's break at any given time, and there were a few years there, where I didn't take a break at all. The times when I did take a rare week off, I always checked my emails while away, called the office to generally let everyone know that I wasn't really on holidays (not *really*), and I was still completely contactable and could be on any necessary conference call that I needed to be, blah, blah, blah ad nauseam here. It's exhausting, just writing that. Shocker, right? Or does that sound familiar to you right now? It probably resonates, and unfortunately, you would be in good company.

So why did I behave this way? Why do you? As a friend of mine pointed out to me the other day, I have always been driven. And I have nearly always been excited about my work, keen to get in there every day, and get on to the next project. But unfortunately, for many years, they were not the reasons why I didn't take my leave. It's a little darker than that. I used to be so fearful that, if I was away for even a millisecond, someone somewhere would realise that they really didn't need me around, they could do quite fine (thank you very much) without me, and I would become irrelevant. What a load to carry, and sad to say, it is a load carried by so many women (and men), you wouldn't be able to count them all. But I have learnt in recent years that it is your talent that makes you indispensible, and it remains the same, whether you are sending that last email at midnight, or sending it at a decent time like 6pm (actually 5pm would be better if we were being real, so you can get to the gym/ home for the kids/out for dinner by 6pm).

In fact, hopefully you now agree after everything you have learned in this book, that your talent will actually thrive, the more frequently you take your breaks. Your talent and the value you add will be fresher and more innovative, when you come back from a few weeks off, than if you stay slogging your guts out for six months straight, without so much as a long weekend to catch your breath.

So, what might breaks look like for you? Well, it will be different for everyone, so it's hard to just give you a list. For me, I like to mix it up a little, and I have learnt that this works really well for me (not a big fan of routine, you see). I have a three-day break every week, from my corporate job at least. Now, I don't sit around on the couch eating cookies for three days. Some would say it's not really their idea of a break at all, as I am working on my book, or wellness stuff, or a potential TV show (exciting!), but I am also doing yoga, and going for walks, and picking up Luca from school, and sleeping in, and yes, watching some good old TV (yes that reality stuff, but you already knew that).

I take medium-sized breaks, at least once during the year. I will head up to Byron Bay and just chill, walk on the beach, do yoga, get a massage and totally veg out. Or I will have a week at home, out of the office, away from other work commitments, and rest, play domestic goddess (have we met?) and enjoy being on retreat, without having to go anywhere.

And then there is the annual break I have been taking for the last three or so years, where I take most of January off. January is a slow month for me work-wise and my son is on vacation, so it's the perfect time to be able to get away from the office, spend time with Luca, and not feel like I am missing important meetings. Some years we have gone to Byron, one year I went overseas while Luca was with his Dad for three weeks, and this year we are here together in North America.

It's an amazing feeling, to be able to switch off from the routine of daily life, when on this type of holiday. No meetings, no conference calls, no weekly food shopping to do (only the fun kind, involving shoes), no cooking or domestics, no school lunches, no homework, nothing of a regular nature to have to contend with. The body and the brain can just let go and relax. And the spirit gets that chance to recharge as well, and find its way home.

For me, changing from the complete workaholic I used to be, to my current state, took a real mindset shift. We have talked about mindset and looked at growth versus fixed mindset and some other aspects. This mindset is a different shift. It's one of permission. Permission you give to yourself. Permission to just be, even if it is just for an evening, to switch off, relax, let go and take a break.

What types of breaks can you build into your weekly life? How about on a monthly basis? What could your annual holidays look like? What are you holding on to that may be limiting your willingness to take the breaks you so desperately need? I invite you to think about how you can build regular breaks into your lifestyle, and see the changes this will make, not only to you, but to those around you too. As with everything, it starts with you, and the ripple of change flows both inward and outward.

Getting real – *remember*

···• No-one likes a martyr, so don't be one. The days of slogging your guts out for endless months without a break, hoping someone will notice, and killing yourself in the process, are over. And if it's not over where you work, go find somewhere else to work, where they respect what your body, mind and spirit need to flourish.

···• Work out how to build frequent breaks into your working schedule – long weekends, a week off every couple of months, and a longer break, of at least a few weeks, once a year. These are all necessary parts of rest and recovery from your busy working life, and will help you to perform at your peak.

···• Breaks are not a luxury – they are a necessity for you to reach your ultimate potential. And you know what they say – all work and no play makes Betty a very boring girl – and no-one wants to be boring!

CHAPTER 35

Build healthy habits, create positive rituals

Motivation is what gets you started.
Habit is what keeps you going.

– Jim Ryun

I n one of my favourite books, *The Creative Habit* by Twyla Tharp, the dancer and legendary choreographer talks about her morning ritual. *I begin each day of my life with a ritual: I wake up at 5.30am, put on my workout clothes, my leg warmers, my sweatshirts, and my hat. I walk outside my Manhattan home, hail a taxi, and tell the driver to take me to the Pumping Iron gym at 91st Street and 1st Avenue, where I work out for two hours. The ritual is not the stretching and weight training I put my body through each morning at the gym; the ritual is the cab. The moment I tell the driver where to go I have completed the ritual. It's a simple act, but doing it in the same way each morning habitualises it – makes it repeatable, easy to do. It reduces the chance that I would skip it or do it differently. It is one more item in my arsenal of routines, and one less thing to think about.*

Ms Tharp goes on to say what we all know – first steps are hard, especially getting up in the pitch black and pulling your tired old body out of bed to go to the gym. We all know this is hard, which is why so many of us don't do it (me included). She also says that the ritual is a friendly reminder that she is doing the right thing – she has done it before, it was good, and she'll do it again.

Rituals are patterns of behaviour that have become automatic. They eliminate the need to think about what to do, how to do it, or whether to do it all. You have pre-programmed yourself, as Nike says, to *just do it.*

My girlfriend Michelle gets up at 5.30am every morning to meditate. Then she goes for a walk to the beach with the sun coming up over the ocean, and then goes home to write. She has been doing this for years and it is a cherished part of her day that is now a ritual for her; and it is the foundation of what a successful day looks like. She once said to me that *she feels like she is walking through mud all day, if she skips her morning routine.*

My Dad gets up every morning to go for a run and a swim. Every day. He is 72, and is one of the fittest people I know, in mind and body. My brother gets up at 4.30am every day to walk 30 minutes down to the beach, where he swims, body surfs and walks on the beach until long after the sun comes up. Before the crowds hit the beach, he is back at his desk working away, having performed his morning ritual.

When I wake up in the morning, I can't get up without doing a few yoga poses in bed. Cat and cow pose and extended child pose are required, before I can put my feet on the floor. Interestingly, my son has taken this ritual to be his own too – one of my good habits he has adopted (we won't talk about the bad ones). Also, before I go to sleep at night, I lie in bed in supta baddha konasana – goddess pose – and do my evening meditation and give thanks for my day. I can't go to sleep without it.

And, of course, there are the rituals that professional athletes perform. You are watching a rugby game, and the guy who is taking the kick at goal will put the ball down in an exact way, then he will walk four steps forward and back three times, tap his legs, pull his ear, and then run to kick the ball, always starting off on the same foot. A tennis player will have a similar ritual when serving, the way she chooses which ball to use, the way she touches her hat, her skirt, tucks the spare ball in her pocket, and how many times she bounces the ball before she throws it in the air. Both athletes have an automatic sequence that removes fear, and replaces it with comfort and routine, and instils confidence.

Healthy habits. Positive rituals. They can be the turning point in becoming the well woman that you know is inside you, waiting to burst out and live the golden life. But it is one thing to just tell you that you need to have them, and another to actually create them. So let's look at what the building blocks are, to create the rituals that will enable your health and wellbeing to take flight. I have my 'top five' list for creating positive habits and rituals, and I share them here. Consider them, try them out, choose the habit that you want to build, and play with these to see what works for you. Remember, it's the initial discipline that is the hardest, and you will build momentum as you keep moving forward. It won't be hard forever.

1. *Pick one thing*

Yes, you heard me right. Pick *only* one thing. I have seen so many people decide to get fit and healthy, and set an intention that looks something like the following: from tomorrow I will cut out all gluten, sugar, dairy, alcohol, and I will work out for 90 minutes every day, meditate for an hour every day, go to sleep by 9.30pm and get up at 5.30am. God, I am tired and demotivated just reading that list! And yes, I have been the guilty one on more than one occasion, and this list has been one of mine. We don't change our whole lives in one day. For goodness sake, be a little gentle on yourself and just pick one. One! Creating any new habit and positive ritual is challenging. We are rewiring the brain here people; this isn't child's play. So never try to commit to creating more than one positive habit at a time.

2. *Commit to* at least *thirty days*

As I mentioned in Chapter 10 when we looked at positive change, the research on habit formation, that tells us 21 days is all it takes to change a deeply-ingrained habit, has been questioned by neuro and behavioural scientists, who think it could actually take upwards of six months. I believe that to be true. However, sticking with something new for a minimum of 30 days gets you through the initial conditioning phase, and makes it much more likely that the new habit will stick. But you have to be – I hate to say it – relentless, for that 30-day period. No ifs, ands or buts.

3. Do it daily

As I said above, we are rewiring the brain here, so you need to practise your new habit frequently and consistently. If you want to meditate or start exercising, do it every day. If you want to have more greens in your diet, get your green smoothie happening every day. If you want to get up earlier, get up at the same time every day. You see the pattern here. If you miss one day, it is a slippery slope, as it just becomes too easy to miss another day, and then another and another. Be consistent, and your new ritual will have a much greater chance of becoming sticky.

4. Be accountable

It is so easy to let yourself off the hook, when you are trying to create a new habit. You intend to start a new healthy eating plan, and while you stuff the cupcake in your mouth on Friday you tell yourself, *Oh, I will start Monday.* Of course you will my love – but Monday of which year? You are only kidding yourself (don't worry gals, I am lecturing myself here). You have to be accountable to yourself for the new habit you have said you will create, and then stick to it. Otherwise your subconscious mind just says, *who is she kidding, I have heard this all before,* and you completely lose confidence in yourself and in your ability to follow through. Write down your commitment, tick off your new habit every day you have achieved success (every day of course), and thank yourself for it. You are worth it, you deserve it, and only you can hold yourself accountable for doing it.

5. Pick your trigger

The trigger to the ritual is what Twyla Tharp talked about in the opening story – she got up, got dressed and got in the cab. Trigger. The ritual was the cab ride, and then the healthy habit just flowed from there. If you want to exercise in the morning but can't get motivated, sleep in your gym clothes and put your alarm on the other side of the room. Once you have to get up to turn off the alarm, and you are already dressed, you may as well get out for your walk. Or if you want to meditate and have quiet reading time at night, but can't motivate yourself to get up from in front of the television, set your alarm again on some horrid tone and put it next to your meditation cushion. You will have to get up to turn it off, and once you are there you may as well sit your fine butt down. Pick your trigger, and you are much more likely to follow through on your habit.

And one final thought – be gentle and kind to yourself. It can sometimes be a challenging process, especially when you are trying to bring in a new habit that counters something you may have been doing your whole life. Be realistic, and treat yourself like you would a friend. Celebrate and treat yourself, when you have a success. And if you mess up, the world won't end, believe me. There is always another day. And we start from where we are.

Getting real – *remember*

···• Think about the one thing that you want to create a healthy habit around, and make a commitment to yourself to stick with it for at least a month. Do it daily, and identify your trigger to ease your success.

···• Find a way to be accountable to yourself – tick your habit off a list at the end of day, put a mark on a calendar, send an email to a friend confirming your achievement. It doesn't matter what it is, just find one that works for you.

···• First steps can be hard, so go easy on yourself, and know that there is always tomorrow, if today wasn't as great as you wanted it to be. New opportunities will arise with the sun, and you can choose to be the person you want to be again tomorrow.

CHAPTER 36

Being the best parent, for you and your kids

There is no single effort more radical in its potential
for saving the world, than a transformation
of the way we raise our children.

– Marianne Williamson

I thought twice about putting in a chapter on parenting in this book, for two reasons. Firstly, I am no expert. You have heard me say that before, but I emphasise it when it comes to this topic. I am blessed to have an amazing, well-rounded, grounded and super cool son, and I am so very lucky to be his mother. Sometimes I look at him wondering where on earth he came from, and how he ended up being so fabulous. Because boy, have I made mistakes. Huge ones. And it's a daily challenge to know that I am doing the right thing, to serve him well in the short and long term. So that was the first reason. The second reason I thought twice, is that I know not everyone reading this book will be a parent. I am acutely aware that 'having it all' is not a conversation and challenge limited to parents, and my intent for this book is to help all women create the career and life they want, regardless of their parenting status. I didn't want it to be perceived otherwise, and I do know it's a touchy subject for many, on both sides of the fence (and anyway, it's time that fence came down, don't you think?).

So, I thought twice. But I decided to include it, as I didn't think I'd be doing justice to those of you out there who are mothers, or want to become one, without writing about what I have learnt about parenting that helps our children flourish (and keeps us sane in the process). And I knew it would also help the aunties, godmothers, and special friends among you, who have wonderful children in your lives. So that is the context. Phew, now on to the stories!

Motherhood. Hardest job in the world? Yes. Most rewarding? For sure. Most undervalued? Maybe. Most pull your hair out, scream at the wall, stick your head in the oven, frustrating job ever designed? Absolutely! You wouldn't give it up for anything, you don't want to miss a single second of their lives, and your heart can feel like it is about to simply burst with love and pride, when they do something just amazing, like smile at you. But it doesn't come without its challenges. And for those working mums among us, it can sometimes seem downright impossible. Now I don't believe in bitching and moaning and complaining about how hard it is. It is what it is, we make choices, and we get on with it. But that doesn't mean we can't talk about the realities.

We have talked about heaps of stuff in this book that will help you as a working mother. Managing your energy, getting the basics right, boundaries, non-negotiables, sleep, restoration, taking your breaks, building healthy habits, and let's not forget, getting happy. They are all keys to your personal success, which of course flows into the success of your family.

But how on earth do you pull it all together? How do you make sure that you are being the best parent, for you and for your kids? I wanted you to hear from two mothers, who I think are just amazing, and I will also share here some of my key learnings on how I make it work (or try to).

The first is Rachael Bermingham, bestselling author of the *4 Ingredients* cookbooks and new book, *Savvy*, and owner of her own publishing company, Bermingham Books. Rachael is also single mother to three boys. I asked Rachael to give us a sneak peek into how she makes it all work.

Juggling three little boys, a business and still maintaining my sanity is certainly challenging at times but thankfully not impossible! I plan and schedule my time, so that each area of my life has the attention it requires. If I stick to the schedule and keep focused in my business by being productive in my work times, then life runs smoothly. It is structured and busy, for sure! However it's how I manage to be the Mum I wish to be and also successfully run my business and manage my team.

I keep things as uncomplicated as possible. My philosophy is, if my boys are fed, get enough sleep, receive enough cuddles and kisses, and get one on one time with me throughout the day and enough activities to keep their minds and bodies active, then they're happy. Children learn most of what they know from their parents and peers, so I concentrate on the way I speak, what I say and how I act as a person, so I can lead by example. It's funny how you hear them repeating what you say or the way in which you say it – they are like little sponges and soak up everything given to them, both positive and negative, so I do my best to BE my best for them.

I wake around 5.30-6am – take a few minutes to be grateful for who and what I have in my life, I check my messages for any urgent ones I have to action straight away (usually from the USA), then have a quick shower before the boys wake up at 6.15-6.30am. Then it's breaky time, I get the boys ready for their day, pack lunches and take Jaxson to school. If it's a work day for me, then a sitter will come around 8am and hang out with the twins until midday. Then I pop them to bed and continue working for another hour or two, then we head off to school to pick Jaxson or go to his after sports activity. Twice a week I do a group personal training session where the boys are welcome to attend — they love hanging out with the other kids and I get my all important exercise time! I believe you can't tell your kids to get active when you're not — PLUS we all just LOVE it! We arrive home around 4.30pm, I cook dinner, we eat, the kids play while I clean up, then it's bath, bottles, book and homework time. By 7.45pm all the kids are in bed and I do a little bit of housekeeping, then I'm back into work by 8.30pm. I normally work through then till about 11pm.

There is a stack of advice I would give to a mum who wants to pursue her career without compromising family life – but one of the most important tips I can share is to plan well, know exactly what you want to achieve, and have a schedule which will help you to keep your momentum, keep you focused and assist you in staying on the right track. It's really my saving grace in a MILLION ways!

I have got to know Rachael over the past few months, and she is a full-on, flat out inspiration to women everywhere. She is one of those women you look at and say to yourself, *well, if she can do it with all of that on her plate, then I can do it too.* Fabulous.

The second story I want to share is from one of my best friends you have already met, Michelle McQuaid. Michelle is mother to two gorgeous boys, Charlie who is six, and Jamie who will soon be two. She lives in Melbourne with her husband Patrick, works as an in demand consultant, and is also undertaking her PhD in organisational play (yep, she is freaky productive). Michelle is an expert in positive psychology, which she applies to organisations, and also to children in schools and other settings, to help kids flourish. I wanted Michelle to share with you what she knows about helping kids to thrive.

Well there's the theory, there's the practice and then there's the reality! The theory goes something like this. By helping your kids to build:

- *positive emotion – emotions like joy, interest, pride, hope, gratitude, serenity and the like*
- *engagement – finding their strengths and using them regularly*
- *relationships – love, empathy and high quality connections*
- *meaning – altruism and a sense of connection to something larger than themselves and*

- *accomplishment – self-regulation, grit and mastery*

And with a good dose of resilience – that not only will they be happy and healthy in life but they'll have all the skills they need to flourish through life's lows and highs.

While leading private schools like Geelong Grammar in Victoria and St Peter's in Adelaide spend a small fortune practising these principles for their students, the good news is there's plenty you can experiment with at home.

Some of the favourites in our house have included:

- *Practising gratitude over dinner by asking each family member: What went well today? It's a sure-fire way to boost positive emotions and keep learning about what's important to each other.*
- *Creating a ritual of meditation to bring a little serenity before bed, where a few minutes of slow belly breathing followed by a short mantra help us unwind for the night. A great book called 'Baby Buddhas' inspired me, but in the end it was as simple as sitting and breathing.*
- *Spotting character strengths in my children – like creativity, kindness, humour, integrity, social intelligence and the like – and using these to motivate them (You're such a kind person, so would you mind helping me put the dishes away?) and to recognise and appreciate them (I can see you've really used your strength of creativity to draw this picture).*
- *Encouraging empathy – catching judgements about other people in conversation – by myself, my husband or my children – and gently challenging these with questions that help us imagine what life might be like for this person. How would our comments make them feel? What might cause them to act the way they're behaving? If it was us, how would we like other people to help? Simple questions can reframe an enemy into a friend.*
- *Nurturing altruism – we have a World Vision brother the same age as our eldest child and encourage him to write letters, draw*

pictures and buy small gifts like stickers. It's been a wonderful way to teach him about other countries and lives less fortunate than his.

- *Praising effort – we try to catch him doing the right thing, rather than the wrong thing. Whenever we do we focus on the effort – rather than the outcome – we try and encourage a mindset of learning and persistence.*

- *Teach resilience – we listen carefully to the stories being told in our house and we help each other challenge our beliefs about ourselves or the world, when they're causing us to lean away from life. By being more aware of these beliefs and the emotions and behaviours they generate, we're able to be more resilient in the face of life's challenges.*

The reality is that on some days we get this so right that I want to burst with pride. And on other days, I catch myself yelling about ungrateful children who never listen and do what they're asked, and want to shrivel up in shame (thank God I've taught them to be resilient!). It's not perfect. It's an attempt to keep doing better. It's the willingness to try and the grace to learn from our success and our failures.

What amazing women, and what wonderful philosophies on parenting and building a caring and nurturing environment for children. So inspiring.

Now what about me I hear you ask? Well, as you know well by now, I am single mum to Luca, who has just hit the pre-teen stage! Pre-teen! When on earth did that happen? So what do I do? Well, not surprisingly, I try and live by many of the philosophies and practices similar to what Michelle outlined here. I have done enough in the wellness, positive psychology and self-development spaces, and also my share of research and reading into what makes kids thrive, to pay special attention to what we do at home and the environment that we create together.

Luca's Dad, David, and I have been divorced since Luca was 18 months old, and we have worked long and hard to build a happy, extended, blended family. And, looking at Luca, I think we have been incredibly successful. No, it has not always been easy. But we have always tried to put Luca's needs first, which anyone who has gone through a divorce will tell you – ain't easy. And there have been plenty of times when we have wanted to throttle each other. But for 90 percent of the time, it works great. Luca has a fabulous stepmother, Jen, and an equally cool brother, John, who is six. Luca spends half of every weekend with them, and half of all the holidays, so there is a nice ebb and flow for him. We also try and do all the school stuff together, and birthdays and other celebrations. It works for us. It's calm, happy and peaceful (well, as peaceful as any Italian Catholic guy and fiery Taurean redhead can be together – you get the picture – we divorced for a reason!).

In terms of the things Luca and I do at home to keep a somewhat calm atmosphere in our daily lives, it varies. We are both fairly organic people – read that to mean that we like organised chaos and aren't very rigid. We don't mind eating dinner on the couch sometimes, neither of us is too concerned with a little bit of mess (to a point), we aren't very structured and we tend to go with the flow as much as possible.

However, there are some things that I am pretty structured about. Homework would be number one. I am not one of those parents that says no TV during the week, or no computer time etc. I have tried that, but it doesn't work for us. Plus, we like to watch some TV together in the evening, it's part of our relaxation time. But homework is king. Yes it's a challenge; we live in the real world and he is a pre-teen boy, come on! But I am pretty relentless on that. Reading is another thing and luckily, if he has a good book, he loves half an hour or more of reading before bed.

Time together not buried in the domesticity of life is really critical to carve out, so that the whole week doesn't just feel like moving from one required thing (school) to another (homework), and a nagging mother (me!), with no fun time in between. Being just the two of us most of the week, we do have a special and close bond, that I am so very grateful for. It's like we are in our own little world, even when there are others in the room. We are a tight little team, and really like hanging out with each other, going to the beach, to the skate park, the movies, out for sushi dinner on Friday nights to our special place, or just chilling out at home, me at my desk writing and him sitting in the armchair next to me on his Mac or reading something. It's pretty chilled most of the time.

We meditate together most nights, and while it is only brief, no more than ten minutes, I think he does it more because we are together, than because he wants to meditate. But he does it, and I know it is laying the way for him to be able to look after himself, his mind and his spirit in years to come. And while I have taught him that it is fine to feel whatever emotion he feels, anger, sadness, frustration or whatever, we try and focus on the positive wherever possible. We always try to have those last moments before sleep filled with wonderful thoughts about all the possibilities in the world, with him knowing just how much he is loved, treasured and adored.

In terms of making it all work, which is the question I possibly get asked more than any other, I do all of the things we have talked about in this book. Literally. In particular, I have gotten especially good at setting really clear boundaries, and managing my non-negotiables. And really importantly, I have lots of support from my family. Luca spends a few afternoons each week with my parents after school, and has done so ever since he has was little, which helps me balance the whole working mother race-from-the-office-juggle-all-those-meetings-without-losing-my-mind thing. And my brother helps out a lot too. I couldn't have done what I have in my career without their love and support, and their really close involvement in Luca's upbringing. I know how blessed I am.

Now, a final word about being the best parent for you and your kids. There's the big thing many mothers don't talk about, but that hopefully you have gotten the gist of by now in this book. You have to look after yourself. Especially as a parent, you have to take care of you before you take care of the kids (and anyone else who needs looking after, husband, pets, house included). Put your own oxygen mask on first. It is a must. You need to bring 'taking care of you' up from the bottom of the list (yes, I know that is where it is, you can't lie to me) and put it on the top.

And we have to lose the guilt that often comes with taking care of ourselves (and everything else to do with being a working mother). In his book, *Find your strongest life: what the happiest and most successful women do differently,* Marcus Buckingham dispels the myth that what school age kids want is more time with their mothers. He says that only ten percent want more time. Their most common request is that they want their mum to be less stressed and tired. Go figure. I think Luca would absolutely agree with that. So lose the guilt, and get yourself to the top of the list. Take that bubble bath. Have a glass of wine. Go to yoga class (not in that order though). Leave the washing to the weekend, or better yet, get your partner or kids to do it. Take off for a weekend retreat with your girlfriends. Paint a picture, read a book, stand on your head if you have to (actually that works a treat). Whatever it takes, take care of you. It has to be one of your non-negotiables, and you have to learn how to do the things we talk about in this book – for your sake and for your families.

Our kids are the most important things in the world to us. Of course they are, and they should be. They are cherished gifts from the heavens, who so luckily chose us as their parents. There are so many things we can do to nurture, nourish and grow them into the wonderful human beings they are destined to be. And we can do that most effectively, and with the most love and care, when we look after ourselves as well.

Getting real – *remember*

···• A few suggested reads from Michelle and me on raising happy, healthy kids are: 'Mindset' by Carol Dweck, and 'The Optimistic Child' by Martin Seligman.

···• There are lots of things you can do to bring peace, calm and positivity into your kids' upbringing. Try out some of the things shared here and see what works for you. Also check out the 'Buddhism for Mothers' series of books by Sarah Napthali for some Zen-like inspiration.

···• Remember, please, to look after yourself first. You can't be the best parent if you are burnt out, cranky, frustrated or over it. Use the information in this book and be kind to yourself, so you can be there for your family, in the way you want to be.

CHAPTER 37

Nurture your spirit, feed your soul

Perfect love casts out fear.

– A Course In Miracles

hen I was about 21, I was given a book that changed my life. The book was *A Return To Love: Reflections on the Principles of A Course in Miracles* and the author was Marianne Williamson. It may sound dramatic to say that it changed my life. It probably is a little. But it did change me. I can't exactly put my finger on it, but it was like my spirit, something I had never really given too much thought to, had been set alight. After reading it, I remember doing routine things like getting the train to work, and just sitting there smiling into space, book on my lap, because I felt like I had discovered this amazing secret, a key to peace and contentment that I had not known existed until then.

Before that, I was pretty busy, you know, partying, working, studying, oh, and did I mention partying? Yeah, I did a lot of that. There was very little that was spirit worthy in my life up until that point. We just weren't in touch with one another. Hey spirit, want another vodka? Hmmm, not quite. But picking up *A Return To Love*, which was sent to me in a humble brown box, alongside a gorgeous black teddy bear, as a present to cheer me up while bedridden with chronic fatigue syndrome, changed all of that. It made me feel something somewhere deep down inside my soul, and ignited a fire – my spiritual fire. They say the teacher appears when the student is ready. I guess I was ready.

The word 'spirit' means different things to different people. For some it is a religious word, which is honoured through going to church and praising God. For some, it doesn't mean much, or it means nothing at all. And for some, like me, it is all about being in touch with something that is bigger than me. I call it universal power. My spiritual life is just that – a way of living from my spirit. And living from my spirit feeds my soul. And hokey as that may sound, it's truly a beautiful thing.

I want to leave you with just a few thoughts in this chapter. And I want to pose a few questions. We have covered so many wonderful things in this book, to help you on your journey of discovery into the best of who you are; how you can love your career; and how you can instil true wellbeing in your life. I hope it has been a worthwhile and insightful journey for you. But how will you know if you are successfully walking the path you have started on? How will you know if it is all working, these things we have uncovered together?

Well, I just have to ask you this question: *How is your spirit?* How do you feel deep down in your soul, in the quiet of the night when no one is around? When you think of your passion, your purpose, your work, your life vision, do they move you? Do they inspire you? Inspire simply means 'in spirit'. When we are inspired, we are in touch and connected at the deepest level. We are doing what moves us beyond words. What we were born to do.

I ask you to consider those questions. And this one – consider how you feel when you are at your most spiritual. For me, it is when I am sitting on my meditation cushion, or on my yoga mat at the end of practice just before namaste. It is when I am burning incense at my desk, or when I see a statue of Buddha in my backyard. It is when I am by the ocean, when I look at the stars, when I watch my son sleeping like an angel. It is when I am connected, deeply, soulfully connected. Connected to something greater than me, connected to truth, to stillness and to peace. It is when I am connected to love.

Where does your inspiration come from? Are you living from that place? Could you be? I know you can. Will you?

Getting real – *try this*

···• Think about when you feel your most connected, the most peaceful, when you feel the most in flow – this is likely when you are inspired and living in touch with your spirit.

···• How can you live from that place? How can you let your spirit be your guide and your constant companion?

···• If you are not feeling connected, that's okay. Just get quiet, dig a little deeper, and seek it out. Your spirit is always with you. Find your inspiration source, and there, you will find your connection.

Nourish the Goddess

Let your light shine. Be a source of strength and
courage. Share your wisdom. Radiate love.

– Wilfred Peterson

So there you have it. *Getting real about having it all: be your best, love your career and bring back your sparkle.* How did you go? How did you feel flowing through the chapters? Were there parts that felt challenging, and others that were a dream come true? I would imagine so. It's all part of the wonderful process of self-discovery, self-development and creating change.

What will you do now that you have finished the book? Go back and do some of the things I recommended? Think about creating that change you have been dreaming about? Go sit and meditate and see what unfolds? Whatever you do, I hope that it is beautiful.

I want to say a heartfelt 'thank you' for coming on this journey with me, and for trusting me to be your guide. We are goddesses. And goddesses deserve to be celebrated, nourished and cherished (and have all the goodness in the entire universe come to us, of course!). I believe that we can create that for ourselves. I also believe that our lives are what we make them. We all have choices, and we choose not only how we want to show up in the world, but we can choose what our world looks like too. It will be what you create. So create something extraordinary.

Until we meet again, I wish you peace and happiness.

Be Well.

Megan xo

Acknowledgements

When I pick up a new book, I always read the acknowledgements first. I am so curious about the author's journey, to see who has been there along the way, and what it has all meant. And now it's my turn.

I must start at the beginning. I have been blessed with the most amazing family. To my parents, thank you does not do justice to all you have done, and all that you are to me. You have been there with your love and support every single step of my life. Thank you for showing me what unconditional love and amazing parenting looks like. And to my brother Jamie, thank you for always being there to help me out, and for being a great uncle.

I have had many fabulous jobs and bosses in my career, but three great men stand out. To the amazing IBM CEOs I have worked for, my heartfelt thanks. To Philip Bullock who gave a fresh-faced IBMer the biggest job of her career, thank you for your belief I could do it, and for giving me the opportunity. To Glen Boreham, thank you for helping me change my life and find the balance I so desperately longed for, for being my friend and a great role model for what matters. And to Andrew Stevens, from the moment we met I just knew I had to work for you, and now, more than a decade later and in a different company, we have come full circle. Thank you for being a truly great mentor and sponsor, and for being a shining example of what positive leadership looks like.

To the fabulous people who lovingly read versions of this book, contributed content, or gave me insightful feedback that shaped the outcome, I thank you – Naomi Wolf, Manuela Schmidt, Rebel Talbert, Sherry Strong, Terry Robson, Jane Horan, Helen Fitzpatrick, Vanessa Auditore, Holly Ransom, Michelle McQuaid, Taren Hocking and Rachael Bermingham. Big love and gratitude.

To my beautiful integrative doctor Marilyn Golden, for your constant love and care. And to Angela Hywood, for getting me through those last six weeks of writing with my energy and sanity in check. Thank you both for being my guiding lights on the wellness path.

To my coach, Vanessa Auditore, I carried your card around in my purse for two years before I came to see you, and life has not been the same since. Thank you for being my soulful guide on the journey to discover my purposeful path. With grace and ease, I thank you.

To my wonderful team at Hay House, thank you for taking a punt on a new author with a big dream. Leon Nacson, thank you for inviting me in to the Hay House family, and for the phone call that would change everything. I am most humbled and grateful. And to Rosie Barry, you have been the best mentor I could have asked for on this unknown journey into the world of publishing. Thank you for your guidance, your support, and for helping me bring my dream and vision to life.

To my many teachers past and present, thank you for the gift of knowledge and inspiration. And to the amazing colleagues and friends who bless my days. You know who you are. Thank you for being there to cheer me on.

To my soul sisters, Taren Hocking and Michelle McQuaid. Taren, you are such a Goddess. Who would have thought way back when at that first SWB event, that we would be where we are now, doing such amazing things together. Your constant belief in my capacity to inspire and empower, and your willingness to share the path with me, is one of the greatest gifts of my life. And to Michelle, a fateful plane trip from Philly to Boston would change our lives. Where would I be without our planning, dreaming and scheming. Thank you for giving me the courage to dream big and for always believing that amazing things are not only possible, but coming (of course!). Without you both, I simply wouldn't be here. I am eternally grateful for our sisterhood.

And to the most important person in my world, my super cool son, Luca. You light up my world, and I thank the universe every day for you. Thank you for choosing me.

I bow in gratitude.

Namaste

We hope you enjoyed this Hay House book. If you'd like to receive our online catalogue, featuring additional information on Hay House books and products, or if you'd like to find out more about the Hay Foundation, please contact:

Hay House Australia Pty. Ltd.,
18/36 Ralph St., Alexandria NSW 2015
Phone: +61 2 9669 4299 • *Fax:* +61 2 9669 4144
www.hayhouse.com.au

Published and distributed in the USA by:
Hay House, Inc., P.O. Box 5100, Carlsbad, CA 92018-5100
Phone: (760) 431-7695 • *Fax:* (760) 431-6948
www.hayhouse.com®

Published and distributed in the United Kingdom by:
Hay House UK, Ltd., 292B Kensal Rd., London W10 5BE
Phone: 44-20-8962-1230 • *Fax:* 44-20-8962-1239
www.hayhouse.co.uk

Published and distributed in the Republic of South Africa by:
Hay House SA (Pty), Ltd., P.O. Box 990, Witkoppen 2068
Phone/Fax: 27-11-467-8904
www.hayhouse.co.za

Published in India by:
Hay House Publishers India, Muskaan Complex, Plot No. 3, B-2,
Vasant Kunj, New Delhi 110 070
Phone: 91-11-4176-1620 • *Fax:* 91-11-4176-1630
www.hayhouse.co.in

Distributed in Canada by:
Raincoast, 9050 Shaughnessy St., Vancouver, B.C. V6P 6E5
Phone: (604) 323-7100 • *Fax:* (604) 323-2600
www.raincoast.com

Take Your Soul on a Vacation
Visit **www.HealYourLife.com**® to regroup, recharge, and reconnect with
your own magnificence. Featuring blogs, mind-body-spirit news, and
life-changing wisdom from Louise Hay and friends.

Visit **www.HealYourLife.com**® today!

CPSIA information can be obtained at www.ICGtesting.com
Printed in the USA
LVOW06s0535220713

343860LV00002B/20/P